*Dedicated to
Mom
and the
American Flag!*

Cookbook Ingredients

It is remarkable how closely the history of the apple tree is connected with that of man.
Henry David Thoreau

An Applelogue

Apples are a favorite American symbol of home, hearth, and happiness. Apple legend and lore have filled volumes. Whether eaten freshly picked from the tree or cooked in any number of ways, apples are a staple of the American diet. Their flavor, availability, versatility, and economy would be enough to account for their popularity; the fact that they are also nutritious comes as a bonus.

Memories of backyard apple trees belong primarily to an earlier generation. But nowadays, in growing numbers, people compensate for the lack by making autumn treks to rural areas for orchard-fresh apples, either buying them at roadside stands or going straight into the orchards to pick their own.

What to do with the bounty? Simply start cooking!

The first edition of the *Apple Orchard Cookbook* was the result of countless hours of mulling over and kitchen-testing a large number of apple recipes, many of which had been entries in several years' worth of apple cooking contests; dozens of them actually are those award-winning selections.

This second edition of the *Apple Orchard Cookbook* increased the number of apple recipes to a hundred plus a generous baker's dozen. Cooking trends and lifestyles change at an ever-increasing pace but the much-loved homespun taste of apples has been retained in these recipes. However, today, more than 30 years since the first printing, "homespun" might just as easily have its roots in India, Mexico, or the Middle East as in rural America.

The recipes range from the familiar, such as Mulled Cider and Apple Crisp, through such old favorites as spareribs transformed into Spicy Apple Ribs Country-Style, to more exotic creations such as Curried Apple and Banana Soup.

You can create a personalized cookbook by including your own family favorites on the Notes pages at the end of each recipe section.

The authors hope that by providing a selection of information, quotes and quips, statistics and tips about apples they are also providing a large measure of enjoyment and amusement for those who use this *Apple Orchard Cookbook*.

ACKNOWLEDGMENTS

The authors are grateful to Boston WCVB-TV's former *Good Day!* program that initiated the 1974 Apple Cooking Contest, co-sponsored by the departments of agriculture of New England states that resulted in this collection's inclusion of several of those award-winning recipes.

The National Agricultural Statistics Service (NASS) of the United States Department of Agriculture provided the updated statistics for apple production in the U.S. The USDA is also the source of the nutritional information regarding apples.

Appreciation is also extended to Betty's husband, Amos, son, Ron, and to Janet's sisters, Elinor Ruth Adler and Joan Louise Eames, for their continuing enthusiasm for this endeavor.

All About Apples

APPLE PICKINGS

Availability

July to August	Early McIntosh, Gravenstein, Yellow Transparent
August to November	Jersey Mac, Ginger Gold, Paula Red
September to December	Empire, Grimes Golden, Macoun, Spartan
September to June	Jonathan, Late McIntosh
October to December	Idared
October to April	Baldwin, Newtown Pippin, Rome Beauty
October to May	Cortland, Golden Delicious, Red Delicious, Rhode Island Greening, York Imperial
November to March	Northern Spy, Stayman
November to May	Winesap
Year-Round	Granny Smith

Uses

All Purpose (eating, salads, and most cooking): Baldwin, Cortland, Empire, Golden Delicious, Granny Smith, Gravenstein, Grimes Golden, Idared, Jonathan, Macoun, McIntosh, Northern Spy, Rhode Island Greening, Spartan, Stayman, Wealthy, Winesap, Yellow Transparent, York Imperial.

Eating: Empire, Idared, Golden Delicious, Granny Smith, Macoun, McIntosh, Newtown Pippin, Northern Spy, Red Delicious, Spartan, Wealthy.

Baking: Baldwin, Cortland, Empire, Granny Smith, Idared, Northwest Greening, Rhode Island Greening, Rome Beauty, Spartan, Stayman, Winesap.

A BASKETFUL OF VARIETIES

Baldwin: A large, yellow-streaked, red apple, with firm flesh. It is crisp and juicy, aromatic, and moderately tart. This is an antique variety, dating back to the mid-eighteenth century. Since it takes about 10 years to bear fruit, and then only biannually, it is not very popular with commercial growers.

Cortland: Usually a medium to large apple, somewhat flat, oval in shape, bright red with some green and yellow. The flesh is firm and white, and the jacket is thin. Particularly good for fresh salad, as the white retains its color longer than other varieties. It is mildly aromatic, mildly acid, and delicate in texture. Excellent for eating, good for baking, and fine for pies and sauces.

Empire: A small to medium variety that tends to be a maroon-red with about 50% green, similar to a McIntosh, but thinner skinned, less susceptible to bruising, and a better keeper. The product of a cross between a Red Delicious and a McIntosh, it is juicy, creamy colored, and mildly tart. It makes for a high-quality dessert apple, but is good for all culinary uses.

Golden Delicious: Generally medium to large with a yellow jacket that is sometimes yellow-green. The stem end is full and round, tapering slightly towards the blossom end, resulting in an elongated oval shape. The velvety skin occasionally has a russet appearance. The flesh is yellowish, fine-grained, and mildly aromatic. It is crisp and tender and tastes sweet and juicy, not acid. It holds its color without browning when exposed to air and is rarely mealy, even when overripe. Good for all uses.

Gravenstein: This apple is an old favorite, with tender, juicy, highly flavorful flesh. Great for applesauce.

Granny Smith: A medium to large, bright to light green apple, sometimes with a pink blush, originated in Australia. Its tart and crisp taste makes it excellent for salads and fresh eating. The tangy flavor comes through when baked or sautéed. Now produced primarily on the West Coast, and available year-round.

Honeycrisp: Produced from a 1960 crop of Macoun and Honeygold. Deep red over a yellow skin and exceptionally crisp and juicy texture. Flesh is cream colored and coarse. Excellent for desserts.

Idared: A cross between a Jonathan and a Wagener. It is a medium to large apple with red coloration and a very smooth, shiny skin. Crisp, but sweet and juicy, its tangy taste mellows at maturity. Excellent for snacks and all culinary uses.

Jonathan: Small to medium in size, solid bright to dark red in color. Slightly tough, thin skin with occasional red veins through yellowish white flesh. Crisp, tender, juicy, very aromatic, moderately tart, and sprightly in flavor. An all-purpose apple.

Macoun: A red-green apple somewhat larger than a McIntosh. This variety is the result of a cross between a McIntosh and a Jersey Black. A very aromatic, flavorful dessert apple with a dark purplish-red or rosy blush over a green ground cover. The high-quality flesh is white and firm, but bruises easily. Excellent for snacks, desserts, and general cooking purposes.

McIntosh: Most frequently a medium-sized apple, fairly symmetrical in shape. The bright red color with occasional greenish-yellow stripes radiates from the stem end or sometimes has a green undertone with large blushed areas of red. This is a thin-skinned apple and the skin separates readily from the flesh, but the skin itself is moderately tough. Inside, the flesh is whitish yellow with occasional faint red veins. It is juicy, crisp, medium acid, very aromatic, and flavorful. A good all-purpose apple, very tender. When you use it for cooking, be careful not to overcook.

Newtown Pippin: Available mostly on the West Coast. Medium to large in size with an angular oval shape; deep green to yellow-green in color, often slightly russeted. Somewhat coarse texture, crisp, moderately tart. A good "keeper"; excellent for cooking. Widely used for commercial processing.

Northern Spy: Grown mostly in the Northeast, the northern Midwest, and eastern Canada. A medium to large apple, with plentiful red stripes over a pale yellow-green undercoat. The flesh is creamy and mellow, aromatic, crisp, and juicy. An excellent apple for all uses; it freezes well.

Northwest Greening and Rhode Island Greening: Available in the East and the Midwest. Medium to large in size, angular oval shape, moderately tart, with firm, crisp texture. First becomes available in October. Good for cooking and baking;

fair for fresh eating. Used by the processing industry.

Red Delicious: Skin is thin, smooth, and protective. The stem end is full and round. It tapers towards the blossom end. Note five distinct "knobs" on the calyx or blossom end—an exclusive for Delicious. Ranges in color from light red with bold stripes and tinges of yellow-green to brilliant red and dark red. The flesh is creamy white and fine-grained; it is sweet, crisp, and juicy, with a mild aroma. Taste is low acid. The color of the flesh oxidizes when exposed to air. Its sweetness, flavor, and juiciness make it a good eating and snacking apple.

Rome Beauty: Medium to quite large in size. Good basic red color, occasionally with greenish yellow stripes. Skin is thick, tough, and smooth. Feels firm and heavy. Flesh is whitish yellow. Taste is medium acid; agreeably mild. Cooking or baking improves flavor. Holds its shape well during cooking; fair for eating.

Spartan: The result of crossing a McIntosh and a Newtown Pippin, it is about the size of a McIntosh. A good dessert apple with an attractive purplish-red skin and very white flesh; crisp, juicy, and flavorful. Particularly good for snacks and salads as well as for general culinary uses.

Stayman: Generally medium to large in size. Slightly elongated oval shape; deep red in color, often with some green undertone showing on the surface. Usually slightly russeted, but this does not affect quality. Moderately tart, full, rich flavor. An excellent all-purpose apple for eating, cooking, or baking.

Winesap: A solid, small to medium, deep red apple. Sometimes looks as if the dark red were lavishly splashed over a yellow-green ground color. The skin is medium thick, leathery, and somewhat oily, which makes it a good keeper. Flesh is yellow, with occasional red veins. Has a coarse, firm texture and spicy aroma, with a sprightly, medium acid, winy taste. Good for eating or cooking.

York Imperial: Medium to large in size, blushed, light to pinkish red and green in color. Shape is lopsided. Skin is thick and bright. Flesh is yellowish in color, firm, crisp, and coarse textured. Taste is mildly tart. Used primarily for commercial processing.

APPLE AREAS

If you want to pick apples, your state Department of Agriculture can usually provide a complete list of orchards that are open to the public for apple picking. Availability of labor and the size of the year's crop may determine just how much and to what extent a particular orchard is open, so invest in a call ahead of time so as not to be disappointed after driving long distances. Prices will vary depending on market demand, but, without question, apple picking is a fun day's activity for the whole family.

The following list indicates those parts of the country that produce the major portion of apples available. The average apple crop of the United States is about 236,990,000 bushels and increasing annually. (In 1977 it was 160 million bushels and in 1992 it was 235 million bushels.) And that does not count the growing markets around the globe (for example, Japan and Chile) for imported apples.

The geographic yields by bushel are:

Washington: 130,952,000; Appalachian Area (Virginia, Pennsylvania, West Virginia, and Maryland): 19,143,000; New York: 31,429,000; Michigan: 28,571,000; California: 6,905,000; New England: 4,045,000; North Carolina: 2,857,000; Ohio, Indiana, and Illinois: 4,455,000; Idaho and Colorado: 1,571,000.

WHAT AN APPLE OFFERS

Fruit is part of the good daily diet recommended by the U.S. Department of Agriculture and nutritionists. Guidelines suggest 2 cups of fruit per day for a 2000-calorie diet. As a 1-cup serving of fruit you can count one of the following: 1 small apple, 1 cup sliced or chopped raw apple, 1 cup applesauce, 1 cup apple juice, 1 cup apple cider, 1/2 cup dried apples.

On various packaged products you may also see printed nutrition labeling such as: 1 medium-sized apple (5.5 ounces) contains 80 calories. Based on a 2000-calorie-a-day diet, the apple also provides the following amounts of the minimum daily requirement (MDR) of these nutrients:

5% potassium
7% total carbohydrate (20% dietary
fiber [5 grams], 16 grams sugar)
2% vitamin A
8% vitamin C
2% iron

Keep in mind that fresh apples and apple cider provide the fiber that clear apple juice does not have.

The apple's reputation as nature's toothbrush is well justified. The nonadherent nature, fibrous texture, and juice content are good for the teeth, gums, and facial muscles. Apples are even known to reduce the incidence of headaches and other illnesses associated with nervous tension, colds, and upper respiratory ailments.

What an apple offers adds up to a whole lot!

GETTING TO THE CORE

Americans love to eat apples by sinking their teeth into the sweet juicy fruit. Europeans prefer to use a fruit knife to slice, and then enjoy. Recipes for cooking with apples often call for them to be sliced, diced, or cooked for applesauce. Here are some of the ways to accomplish the task.

To slice: First remove the blossom end (opposite the stem) and then slice vertically around the apple. Be sure that the knife is reaching the core each time. There is a gadget called a slicer/corer that does the job in a jiffy. Note: for pies, peel the apples; for fried apples, leave them unpeeled. The metal blade of a food processor can also slice, but be sure not to overslice or you might end up with mush.

To dice: Cut apple into slices vertically, as above, but do not remove them from the core yet. Now cut into the apple horizontally about every half inch or less. Do this over a board or bowl so that the resulting cubes fall where you want them. Repeat the process for any of the apple that remains.

For sauce: Wash and quarter (with or without skin). Add a small amount of water (about 2 tablespoons per apple) and simmer. Optional additions (singly or in combination) are sugar, brown sugar, ground cinnamon or cinnamon stick, the peel of a quarter of a lemon or less, a bit of butter. When the apples are tender, pour them into a sieve or food mill placed over a bowl or pan. If you use a food mill, alternately turn the handle clockwise and counterclockwise until only skin and seeds remain. This process extracts more apple; it also adds flavor. And if you have left the peel on, its presence adds a touch of color to the sauce. When using a food processor with the metal blade, add apple quarters, no more than eight at a time. Puree and repeat until all apples are used. Be careful not to over-process and liquefy the sauce.

English star-cut: This technique is recommended when apple slices are to be served for dipping or simply for eating raw. To make attractive one-bite segments of apple, hold the apple and slice it through horizontally. You will now have two halves with the core cross-sectioned and usually showing the pattern of a five-pointed star. Divide each half into five pieces, cutting along one of the points to the center, and then along an adjacent point so each segment is removed. Pare out the core from the top of each segment without wasting any of the flesh. The five bite-sized pieces are perfect for decorative arrangements, in salads, or for fondue dipping.

APPLE TREATS

Thrifty Apple Skin Jelly

Use every bit of the orchard's bounty! When peeling apples for pie, sauce, or other dishes, discard stem and blossom ends or any bad spots; place skins and cores in a saucepan. Add 1 cup cold water, cook over low heat for 25 minutes, and strain the juice into cup. (From 4 apples, there should be about 1/4 cup.) If there is too much juice, boil it down to 1/4 cup; if too little, add water to skins until just 1/4 cup juice is obtained. Return the juice to the saucepan and add 3 tablespoons sugar; stir over low heat until sugar is dissolved. Boil rapidly for 1 or 2 minutes, testing constantly until the jelly sheets from a spoon. Pour into a glass jar, and refrigerate when cool, or use as glaze for an open pie or tart.

Frozen Apples

It's easy! Core and peel apples. Slice into twelfths or sixteenths directly into a brine solution of 2 tablespoons salt to one gallon cold water. Blanch in steam for 90 seconds (preferred method), or in boiling water for 60 seconds. Chill in cold water; drain. Sprinkle 1/2 cup sugar evenly over each quart (about 1 1/2 pounds) apples; stir and let stand until sugar is dissolved. Pack into containers, leaving about 1/2 inch space under the cover. Freeze.

Apple Leather (Dried Fruit Roll)

A delectable snack! Use ripe or overripe apples; peel if desired, then core and cut into chunks. Puree in a food chopper or blender. For a lighter color, add one tablespoon of lemon or lime juice for each quart of fruit. Line a cookie sheet or tray with wax paper and pour in the blended fruit about 1/4 inch deep. Set oven at its lowest temperature (140 degrees); place trays inside and leave the oven door open from 2 to 6 inches. The apple leather will be dried in 4 to 5 hours. Enjoy as a snack, or create a beverage by adding 5 parts water to 1 part apple leather in a blender.

TO MICROWAVE AN APPLE

With the presence of microwave ovens in so many of today's kitchens, here are a few words of guidance. Being able to save up to four times of regular cooking time is worth a few extra moments of caution at the start: be sure to read your own oven's manual carefully for specific uses.

Most recipes can be at least partially adapted for microwaving. However, those that require browning of some or all ingredients are still best left for a stove top or a conventional oven. Even though many microwaves now have browning elements, greater success still seems to be achieved the old-fashioned way. Some recipes can be started in the microwave and finished in a conventional oven to get the desired browning or crispiness. Dishes requiring water absorption, such as pasta and rice, take the same amount of time regardless of the type of oven, so select the method that is the most convenient or efficient for whatever you are making.

To bake apples in the microwave, allow approximately 4 minutes per medium-sized apple. (Remember that the more you bake, the longer the cooking time.) Be sure to core the apples first, removing all the seeds; slice off the bottom stem so that the entire apple will be edible when it is done. Pour 1 tablespoon water or apple juice over each apple and cover with wax paper. Bake them plain for a nutritious low-calorie appetizer or dessert. Or, to embellish them, stuff the cavity with any of the following or a combination of these ingredients: maple syrup/chutney, jelly, chopped nuts, cinnamon and sugar, butter, brown sugar, or—you decide!

And of course, a microwave will hasten defrosting and rewarming frozen foods—such as your own homebaked pies! Finishing off a pie for several minutes in a conventional oven at 350 degrees, if desired, makes a crust crispier.

A TIME FOR TASTING

Wine-tasting and cheese-tasting parties have increased people's interest and taught their tastebuds to discern the often subtle differences within groups of foods. Apples lend themselves to a unique taste test that has all the makings of a terrific party. Serve apple drinks, appetizers, and desserts to complement the theme. Copy the information about the various characteristics onto cards which you place alongside a plate of each variety of apple.

To proceed with the taste test, do the following:

1. Place one whole apple of each variety on a large plate.
2. Cut another apple of the same variety into 8 to 10 pieces. Place on the same plate as the whole apple.
3. Look at the whole apple, noting size, shape, color, symmetry. Smell the apple, wafting it gently under your nose. Does it have a characteristic aroma?
4. Look at the cut apples, noting the color of the flesh. Is it snowy white? Creamy? Translucent? Is the peel thick? Leathery? Thin?
5. Bite into a slice of each variety. Is it tart? Savor the juice. Is it sweet? Slightly sour? Is the skin tender or tough?
6. Is the texture tender? Crisp? Mellow? Mealy? Hard?
7. Which variety has the most flavor? The most aroma?
8. Note the color of the cut slices after they have been exposed to the air for a few minutes. Does the flesh of some varieties stay white longer than that of others?
9. Which varieties would be best for salads and fruit cups? Which would you like to serve with meat dishes? Which for desserts?
10. Which varieties would combine best for pies and sauces?
11. Which variety do you prefer to eat out of hand?

APPLE PANTRY NOTES

For the sake of simplicity, we have avoided repeating some fairly obvious options from one recipe to the next. So, please note the following:

1. Unless a recipe specifically states otherwise, medium-sized apples are appropriate.

2. Generally speaking, apples should be cored and peeled. If peels are to be left on, the recipe will say so.

3. When butter is given as an ingredient, you can of course substitute margarine, keeping in mind that the flavor of the more delicate pastries may be affected.

4. When the instructions say to "butter" a baking dish or other utensil, you can usually substitute vegetable shortening. Again, flavor is a factor to consider.

5. For the more or less generic "vegetable oil," you may be able to substitute (in savory recipes) olive oil or (in any of the recipes) some other light-flavored oil such as corn oil or canola oil.

6. When flour is given as an ingredient, we mean all-purpose white flour, sifted once. (Always sift flour first, then spoon gently into the measuring cup.) If another kind of flour, such as whole wheat, is required, the recipe will call for it specifically.

7. Brown sugar is always measured by packing it firmly into the measuring cup or spoon.

8. Unless otherwise instructed, always preheat the oven to the correct baking temperature.

APPLETIZERS

Dips
Hors d'Oeuvre
Soups
Beverages
Snacks

Apple Dipper

1 (8-ounce) package cream
    cheese, softened
3 or 4 tablespoons apple juice
    or cider
1/2 cup grated apples
2 teaspoons chopped chives
Pinch of salt

1. Combine cream cheese and apple juice until smooth and creamy. Blend in well the grated apples; stir in chives and salt to taste. Chill.

2. Serve with carrot and celery sticks, radish roses, apple wedges, and other fresh fruit, vegetables, and crackers as desired.

Yield: About 1-1/2 cups dip.

Carbonized remains of apples found by archaeologists in prehistoric lake dwellings in Switzerland are presumed to be a relic of the Iron Age.

Fruit Curry Dip

2 cups sour cream
3/4 cup (8-ounce can)
   crushed pineapple, drained
2/3 cup chopped red apples
1 teaspoon curry powder
1/2 teaspoon garlic salt
Apple slices (garnish)

1. Blend sour cream with pineapple, apples, curry powder, and garlic salt.

2. Chill. Garnish with apple slices around the edge of the bowl. Especially good with shredded-wheat wafers.

Yield: About 3 cups.

---

*In Herefordshire, Devonshire, and Cornwall, England,
the old custom of "Wassailing" the apple orchards
on Christmas Eve still persists. The farmers
walk in procession to a chosen tree in
each orchard where an incantation
is spoken and a bowl of cider
dashed against the trunk of
the tree, thus ensuring
a fruitful harvest.*

Sausage and Apple Appleteasers

1 (8-ounce) package Crescent
    Dinner Rolls
2 tablespoons melted butter
2 apples, finely chopped
6 slices bacon, cooked until
    crisp; crumbled
8 Brown 'N Serve Sausage
    Links

1. Separate Crescent Dinner Rolls dough into four rectangles; press perforations to seal. Brush each rectangle with butter.

2. Combine chopped apples and crumbled bacon. Spread some of the mixture over the dough. Cut each rectangle crosswise to form two squares. Place a sausage link on each square; roll up. Cut each roll into three or four bite-size pieces; secure with a wooden toothpick. Place cut side down on an ungreased cookie sheet.

3. Bake at 375 degrees for 12 to 15 minutes or until golden brown.

Yield: 24 to 32 appetizers.

Note: If you do not wish to cut the rolls you may use them sandwich size.

Don't pluck a green apple;
when it is ripe it will
fall by itself.
Russian Proverb

Cheese Appletizers

Pastry:
2 cups grated sharp cheddar
    cheese
1 cup butter
2-1/2 cups flour

Filling:
6 cups chopped apples
1/2 cup granulated sugar
1/2 cup light brown sugar
1 tablespoon frozen orange
    juice concentrate
1/3 cup flour

1. For Pastry: Have cheese and butter at room temperature. Cream together until smooth; gradually add flour and mix well. Shape dough into four balls and wrap. Chill.

2. For Filling: Combine all ingredients in a saucepan. Cook over low heat until thickened. Cool before using.

3. On a floured board, roll each section into a 12x6-inch rectangle. Spread one quarter of the filling over half of each rectangle and fold over to make a 6-inch square. Cut each into sixteen 1-1/2-inch squares.

4. Bake on an ungreased cookie sheets at 300 degrees for 20 to 25 minutes or until just barely browned along the bottom edges. Serve hot or cold.

Yield: About 5 dozen appetizers.

Apples are a member of the rose family.

Julia's Danish Herring

1 (12-ounce) jar of marinated
    herring with onions
1/4 cup vegetable oil
1/4 cup tomato paste
1/2 cup chopped Granny
    Smith apple
1/4 cup brown sugar

Cut herring into 1/2-inch squares or bits. Mix all ingredients. Refrigerate for 24 hours. Serve with crisp crackers or rounds of rye or pumpernickel bread.

Yield: 2-1/2 cups.

 FAST APPLE FAVORITE

Apple Salsa Dip

1 (8-ounce) jar Mexican
    chunky-style salsa, hot
    or medium
1 Granny Smith or McIntosh
    apple, chopped
1/2 cup mayonnaise
1/2 cup sour cream

Combine ingredients. Chill and use as a dip with tortilla chips or fresh carrot sticks and celery sticks.

Yield: 2-1/2 cups.

Note: To turn the dip into a salad dressing, add an additional 1/2 cup of mayonnaise.

Swedish Ham Balls

2-1/2 pounds ground ham
1 cup chopped apples
2 cups bread crumbs
2 eggs, well beaten
3/4 cup milk

Sauce:
1 cup brown sugar
1 teaspoon dry mustard
1/2 cup vinegar
1/2 cup water

1. Combine ham, apples, bread crumbs, eggs, and milk in a large bowl; mix thoroughly. Form into small balls and place into a 9x13-inch baking pan.

2. **For Sauce:** Mix together the sauce ingredients; stir until sugar dissolves. Pour this sauce over the ham balls.

3. Bake at 325 degrees for 1 hour. Baste frequently.

Yield: 5 dozen hors d'oeuvre-size or 32 large ham balls.

The apple pressed with specious cant
Oh! What a thousand pities then
That Adam was not Adamant.
Thomas Hood, A Reflection

Zesty Hors d'Oeuvre

1 (3-ounce) package cream
    cheese, softened
1/4 cup crumbled blue cheese
1/2 cup crushed cornflakes
1 cup finely chopped apples
1/4 teaspoon sugar
1/4 teaspoon cinnamon
1/4 cup ground walnuts
4 slices bacon, cooked until
    crisp; crumbled

1. Mix the cheeses together. Add 1/4 cup of the crushed cornflakes and the apples, sugar, cinnamon, walnuts, and bacon; mix well.

2. Shape into small balls. Roll balls in remaining 1/4 cup crushed cornflakes. Chill. Serve on toothpicks.

Yield: About 20 balls.

The signers of the Declaration of Independence toasted their achievement with apple cider and brandy from orchards already a century and a half old.

Curried Apple and Banana Soup

2-1/2 cups vegetable stock
3 to 4 apples, coarsely grated
1 large very ripe banana,
    peeled
1 onion, coarsely chopped
1 tablespoon curry powder
Pinch of salt
1 large potato, peeled and
    finely diced
1 pint light cream, scalded
Chopped chives (garnish)

1. Place 1-1/4 cups of the vegetable stock in a blender with apples, banana, onion, curry powder, and salt. Blend to a smooth puree. (If you do not have a blender, use a food mill or a sieve.)

2. In a large saucepan, combine the puree, potato, and the remaining 1-1/4 cups stock. Bring to a boil; reduce heat and simmer, covered, for 15 minutes or until potato is tender.

3. Place soup in a blender and blend until as smooth as possible. Add scalded cream to the soup, pouring it through a sieve. Stir to blend. Chill. Garnish with chives.

Yield: About 6 cups, or 10 to 12 servings.

Note: To make 1 gallon homemade vegetable stock, combine 5 stalks celery, diced; 3 large carrots (with tops if possible), diced; 1 large onion with skin, quartered; 3 parsnips, sliced; and 2 gallons water in a large pot. Add one bunch each of fresh parsley and dill (or substitute parsley flakes and dill seed). Bring to a boil; simmer, covered, for 1 hour or until reduced by half. Strain.

Superb Scandinavian Apple Soup

2 cups chicken broth
1 tablespoon cornstarch
3 cups diced apples
1/2 teaspoon cinnamon
Dash of salt
1/2 cup sugar
1/2 cup sweet red wine
3 to 4 drops red food
    coloring (optional)
Whipped cream (garnish)
Cinnamon (garnish)

1. Stir together the chicken broth and cornstarch. Combine with the diced apples, cinnamon, and salt in a saucepan and simmer for about 25 minutes or until apples are soft. Pass through a strainer. Add sugar, red wine, and food coloring.

2. Taste for sweetness (this will depend on the kind of apples used) and add more wine or sugar if needed. Chill well.

3. Top each serving with a dab of whipped cream and sprinkle with cinnamon.

Yield: 4 to 6 servings.

Nearly all apples available after harvest time in the fall come from refrigerated storage.

Mulled Cider

1 quart apple cider or apple
   juice
1 teaspoon whole allspice
1 teaspoon whole cloves
2 sticks of cinnamon
6 thin lemon slices (optional)

1. Combine all the ingredients, except the lemon slices, in a saucepan. Simmer, covered, for 20 minutes.

2. Remove spices. Serve hot with lemon slices, if desired.

Yield: 6 servings.

Planting the trees that would march and train
On in his name to the great Pacific,
Like Birnam Wood to Dunsinane,
Johnny Appleseed swept on.
Vachel Lindsay, In Praise of Johnny Appleseed

Apple Cinnamon Cheesies

2 (8-ounce) packages
    Crescent Dinner Rolls
4 slices American cheese,
    each cut into four
    triangles
3 McIntosh apples, thinly
    sliced
3 tablespoons sugar
1 teaspoon cinnamon

1. On a cookie sheet, separate Crescent Dinner Rolls as directed. On each triangle (near the bottom), place a triangle of cheese. Arrange apple slices on top of cheese.

2. Combine sugar and cinnamon and sprinkle mixture over each. Roll up gently as you would normally for Crescent Dinner Rolls.

3. Bake at 350 degrees for 15 or 20 minutes or until golden brown.

Yield: *16 rolls.*

Apples are said to help insomniacs. When you can't fall asleep, try an apple; it will take the blood from the brain and help you get restful sleep.

Notes

APPLE ENTRÉES

Meat
Poultry
Seafood
Dairy

Spicy Apple Ribs Country-Style

2 pounds country-style
  spareribs
1 bay leaf
Water
4 apples, cut in chunks
2 tablespoons honey
1 teaspoon vinegar
2 cloves garlic, minced
2 tablespoons tomato
  ketchup
Paprika to taste

1. Place ribs in a saucepan with water to cover. Add bay leaf. Bring to a boil and simmer about 5 minutes.

2. In a saucepan, combine apple chunks with remaining ingredients, cooking until a smooth sauce is formed.

3. Drain ribs and place on a rack in a roasting pan. Roast ribs at 350 degrees for about 20 minutes.

4. Spoon some of the apple mixture on each rib and continue roasting, turning the ribs a few times and brushing with the apple mixture each time you turn them.

Yield: 2 to 4 servings.

Notes: Can also be cooked without Step 1. Ribs can be marinated in the apple mixture, then cooked in foil on a grill or over charcoal for about 1 hour. Apples can be pureed in a blender if you like.

McIntosh Country Meat Loaf

Meat Loaf:
2 pounds ground beef
1 cup fresh bread crumbs
1 egg, beaten
1 large apple, grated
1/3 cup finely chopped
   onion
1/3 cup finely chopped
   celery (optional)
1/4 cup molasses
Salt and pepper to taste
1/4 cup milk (about)
1 large apple, cut in eighths

Glaze:
2 tablespoons ketchup
2 tablepoons molasses
1 teaspoon mustard

Sauce:
1 cup sour cream
1 tablespoon horseradish
1 grated apple
Salt and pepper to taste

1. For Meat Loaf: Mix all ingredients except milk and apple pieces; blend well. Slowly add enough milk to make mixture moist but not wet.

2. Place in a 9x5-inch loaf pan; top with apple pieces. Bake at 350 degrees for 1 hour. Remove from oven.

3. For Glaze: Combine ingredients and pour over meat loaf. Bake for 15 minutes longer.

4. For Sauce: Combine ingredients. Chill well.

Yield: 1 meat loaf.

Improve the flavor of any cake and make it even more moist by grating a small apple into the batter.

Spicy Beans and Beef

3 slices bacon
1 large onion, sliced
1 stalk celery, sliced
1 pound ground beef
1 (10-3/4-ounce) can cream
    of tomato soup
1 (16-ounce) can red kidney
    beans, drained
1 tart apple, chopped
2 tablespoons brown sugar
Salt and pepper to taste
1 tart apple, sliced

1. Cook bacon in a large, heavy skillet until nearly crisp; remove, drain, and set aside.

2. In bacon drippings, sauté onion and celery until soft and golden, but not brown. Add ground beef, broken up, and cook until browned, stirring often.

3. Remove from heat; add tomato soup, kidney beans, chopped apple, brown sugar, and salt and pepper.

4. Place in a 1-1/2-quart casserole; arrange bacon strips and apple slices on top. Bake at 350 degrees for about 25 minutes. Serve with salad and cornbread for a tasty and economical dinner.

Yield: 5 to 6 servings.

---

*If an apple turns brown near the core, that indicates
it has been stored at too low a temperature.*

Sugar-and-Spice Pot Roast

4 pounds beef shoulder
    pot roast
3 onions, diced
2 cloves garlic, minced
1 stalk celery, diced
1 carrot, diced
2 apples, diced
1 teaspoon salt
2 cups tomato juice
2 tablespoons brown sugar
10 gingersnaps

1. Heat a heavy pot and brown the meat evenly on all sides.

2. Add remaining ingredients and simmer for about 1-1/2 hours or until the meat is tender.

Yield: 6 to 8 servings.

Remember Johnny Appleseed,
All ye who love the apple;
He served his kind of word and deed,
In God's Grand Greenwood Chapel.
William Henry Venable, Johnny Appleseed

Roast Lamb with Apples

3-pound boneless sirloin
    lamb roast
1/2 lemon
2 medium to large apples,
    sliced
8 prunes, halved and pitted
1 tablespoon sugar
2 to 3 cloves garlic, sliced
1 tablespoon ginger
Salt and pepper to taste
1 tablespoon vegetable oil
2 cups apple cider or juice

1. Rub the lamb on all sides with the juice of the lemon.

2. Arrange apple slices and prune halves symmetrically on the meat. Sprinkle with sugar. Roll the meat up carefully and tie with string; skewer if necessary.

3. Using a thin knife, insert garlic slices under the top skin of the meat. Rub skin with a mixture of ginger, salt, and pepper. Brush with oil until the spices adhere to the meat.

4. Heat apple cider or juice and use to baste the meat every 15 minutes or so. Cook for about 20 minutes to the pound to desired doneness. (Delicious when served slightly pink.)

5. Serve with a gravy prepared from the pan juices. Slice carefully so the filling remains in the center when served.

Yield: About 9 servings.

---

*Sweet apples take just about twice as long to cook
as tart, juicy apples.*

Applesauced Pork Chops

4 lean pork chops
2 tablespoons butter, melted
1/2 cup diced onions
3 pieces toast, diced
3 apples, diced
1 (16-ounce) jar applesauce
Dash of nutmeg
3 pinches of pepper
1/2 cup apple wine or
　　apple juice

1. Place pork chops in a roasting pan; cover with melted butter. Top with remaining ingredients.

2. Bake at 400 degrees for 30 minutes. Reduce temperature to 300 degrees and bake for 30 minutes longer.

Yield: 4 servings.

Note: Chops may be browned first, if desired. If you prefer to use homemade applesauce, the quantity needed is 2 cups.

The apples on the other side of the wall are the sweetest.
W.G. Benham, Proverbs

Apple and Sausage Quiche

1-1/4 cups chopped apples
1 tablespoon lemon juice
1 tablespoon sugar
1 small onion, chopped
3 tablespoons butter
6 pork link sausages
4 eggs
2 cups sour cream
1/8 teaspoon nutmeg
Salt and pepper to taste
9-inch pie shell*
1 cup grated cheddar or
    Swiss cheese

1. Sprinkle apples first with lemon juice and then with sugar; sauté with onion in butter until soft but not mushy. Remove from heat and let cool for 20 minutes. Meanwhile, cook sausages and set aside to cool.

2. Beat eggs well; blend in sour cream. Add nutmeg, salt, and pepper. Stir in apple mixture and pour into the pie shell. Sausages may be cut into small pieces and combined with the filling, or arranged on top, pinwheel fashion.

3. Bake at 350 degrees for 45 to 60 minutes, or until a knife inserted in the center of the filling comes out clean. Sprinkle with grated cheese about halfway through the baking time.

4. Let cool for 5 minutes, then cut in wedges.

Yield: 1 quiche (about 8 servings).

*Baked at 400 degrees for about 8 minutes.

Apple and Knockwurst Supper

4 links knockwurst
2 medium onions, chopped
3 teaspoons butter
3 apples, chopped
1/2 cup chicken broth
1/2 teaspoon cinnamon
3 tablespoons brown sugar
Salt and pepper to taste

1. Boil knockwurst in water for 10 minutes. Drain and set aside.

2. Sauté onions in butter just until transparent. Add knockwurst and fry, covered, for 10 minutes.

3. Add apples, chicken broth, cinnamon, sugar, salt, and pepper. Simmer for 15 minutes. Serve with salad and baked potatoes, if desired.

Yield: 2 servings.

---

*The finished man of the world must eat
of every apple once.*
Ralph Waldo Emerson, The Conduct of Life

Chicken Pomme Florentine

2 pounds boneless, skinless
    chicken breasts
4 ounces cheddar cheese,
    thinly sliced
1 (10-ounce) package fresh
    spinach, washed
Butter
2 cups apple juice
1 large tart apple, cut in
    wedges
Dash of nutmeg
Salt and pepper to taste
1 cup rice (optional)

1. Cut chicken breasts into eight similar-sized pieces; flatten with a wooden mallet or rolling pin.

2. Place a layer of cheese slices on each piece of chicken. Top each with small pieces of spinach, roll each up tight, and skewer with toothpicks on uneven side.

3. Sauté the chicken rolls in butter, smooth side down, in a heavy pan over medium heat until lightly browned.

4. Add apple juice and cook over low heat for 20 to 25 minutes. (Add rice now or 5 minutes later, depending on package directions.) About halfway through cooking time, add apple wedges and sprinkle chicken with seasonings.

Yield: 4 to 6 servings.

Notes: Use looseleaf spinach if available. Leave apples unpeeled for a little extra color. Can be cooked in a microwave; times will vary with the size of the chicken rolls.

Chicken Apple Amandine

6 chicken breasts
8 tablespoons butter
2 tablespoons vegetable oil
Salt and pepper to taste
3 tablespoons chopped
    scallions
4 large apples, cubed
1-1/2 cups all-purpose cream
3 tablespoons sliced roasted
    almonds

1. Brown chicken breasts in 4 tablespoons of the butter and the oil.

2. Add salt, pepper, and scallions and simmer for about 30 minutes.

3. Meanwhile, in a separate skillet melt remaining 4 tablespoons butter; add apples and cook for about 10 minutes.

4. When chicken is cooked through and tender, add apples and cream, and cook a few more minutes. Sprinkle with almonds. Serve with rice, if desired.

Yield: 6 servings.

Baked Chicken Barbecue

8 chicken breast halves or
    8 legs (or 4 of each)
Salt and pepper to taste
1/2 cup melted butter
1-1/2 cups chili sauce
1/3 cup water
2 medium onions, sliced
1/3 cup brown sugar
1/2 cup raisins
2 teaspoons Worcestershire
    sauce
6 apples, sliced

1. Rub chicken with salt and pepper. Brush with butter and broil lightly on both sides.

2. Combine chili sauce, water, onions, sugar, raisins, and Worcestershire sauce. Pour over chicken in a shallow baking pan; cover with foil.

3. Bake at 325 degrees for about 50 minutes, or until chicken is cooked through. Add apples during the last half hour of baking time.

Yield: 6 to 8 servings.

Note: This dish can be prepared in advance, omitting the apples, and refrigerated. Add the apples when reheating.

---

*Thirty-five states provide the right conditions
to grow apples commercially.*

Clara's Cider Chicken

3 pounds chicken, cut up
2 tablespoons butter
1/4 cup onions, finely
   chopped
1/4 cup carrots, finely
   chopped
1/2 cup mushrooms, finely
   chopped
1 cup apples, finely
   chopped

1 tablespoon flour
Bouquet garni (1 bay leaf;
   1/2 teaspoon each
   parsley, thyme, and
   tarragon)
1-1/2 cups apple cider or
   apple juice
1 cup light cream
Parsley for garnish
   (optional)

1. Brown chicken well in butter in a large, heavy pot.

2. Add vegetables, apples, flour, and bouquet garni. Pour in cider. Cover and cook for 20 to 30 minutes or until chicken is cooked through.

3. Remove chicken and add cream to the liquid in the pot; simmer until sauce is reduced and thickened. Return chicken to sauce to be sure it is hot. Serve chicken pieces individually, or arrange on a platter and pour sauce over all. Garnish with parsley, if desired.

Yield: About 6 servings.

Shrimp Curry 02159

1 medium onion, chopped
1 Granny Smith apple,
    chopped
2 cloves garlic, crushed
1/4 cup vegetable oil
1/4 cup flour
1 teaspoon salt
1/4 teaspoon pepper
1/2 teaspoon ground ginger
1/2 teaspoon ground
    nutmeg
2 sprigs fresh parsley,
    chopped
20 peppercorns, crushed

1 bay leaf
1-1/2 tablespoons curry
    powder
1 (8-ounce) can stewed
    tomatoes
2 cups water
1/2 teaspoon mustard seeds
2-1/2 teaspoons dried
    cilantro
1 teaspoon fresh lemon juice
1 pound or more medium to
    large cooked shrimp
1/2 cup honey-roasted
    peanuts (optional)

1. Sauté onion, apple, and garlic in oil until onion is transparent.

2. Remove from heat and blend in flour.

3. Add remaining ingredients, except shrimp and peanuts, and simmer for 15 minutes.

4. Remove bay leaf and mix in cooked shrimp and peanuts. Serve over saffron or white rice.

Yield: 4 to 6 servings.

Lemon juice added to apples will intensify their flavor.

Curried Shrimp in Seafood Shells

3 tablespoons butter
1-1/2 cups apples, diced
2 teaspoons curry powder
2 tablespoons flour
1-3/4 cups milk
1 teaspoon salt
1/2 teaspoon onion salt
Dash of nutmeg (optional)

2 cups shrimp, peeled and
    deveined (cut up if
    large)
2 hard-cooked eggs, cut in
    large pieces
1/4 cup melted butter
3/4 cup Italian seasoned
    bread crumbs

1. Melt 3 tablespoons butter in a saucepan; add apples and cook over low heat for about 15 minutes until very tender.

2. Sprinkle with curry powder and flour; cook and stir for a few minutes. Add milk gradually, blending well. Add seasonings and continue cooking until apples soften to sauce texture and mixture thickens.

3. Add shrimp and eggs. Distribute the mixture among 4 to 6 seafood shells or ramekins, or spoon into a shallow baking dish.

4. Stir 1/4 cup melted butter and bread crumbs together until butter is well distributed; sprinkle on top of shrimp mixture. Bake at 350 degrees for 15 to 20 minutes or until golden and piping hot. Serve with rice and fresh mushrooms and chives, and a salad, if desired.

Yield: 4 to 6 servings.

---

*It takes as much as a decade for an apple tree
to start bearing fruit.*

Seafood Apple Casserole

6 apples, diced
1/2 cup butter
1/2 pound shrimp
1/2 pound scallops
2 cloves garlic, finely diced
1-1/2 cups cooked rice
1/2 cup apple cider
Salt and pepper to taste
1/2 tablespoon paprika
3 sprigs fresh parsley
    (garnish)

1. Sauté apples over medium heat in 2 tablespoons of the butter until soft. Puree apples.

2. Sauté shrimp, scallops, and garlic over medium heat in another 2 tablespoons butter for about 7 minutes.

3. Spread rice evenly in a 9x13-inch baking pan. Spread apple puree evenly on top of rice; add apple cider. Arrange shrimp and scallops over rice; pour over them the butter used for cooking them. Add seasonings. Melt remaining 1/4 cup of butter and pour over all.

4. Bake at 350 degrees for 30 minutes. Garnish with parsley.

Yield: 4 servings.

Note: Onions may be added for additional flavor while apples are being cooked. Fillet of sole may be used instead of shrimp and scallops. Lemon slices may be used as a garnish.

Apple Dolmas

1/2 cup chopped onion
1 tablespoon butter
1 cup beef or chicken
bouillon
1/2 cup rice, uncooked
1/2 cup Grape-Nuts
2 teaspoons dried basil
1/4 cup chopped parsley,
or 2 tablespoons dried
parsley

1 pound ground beef
1-1/2 teaspoons salt
Scant 1/4 teaspoon black
pepper
12 small or medium apples
Yogurt (optional)

1. Soften onion in butter over low heat. Add bouillon (1 bouillon cube dissolved in 1 cup boiling water) and bring to a boil. Add rice; cover, reduce heat to low. Cook for 15 minutes or until water is absorbed.

2. Remove from heat; add Grape-Nuts, basil, and parsley. Mix well and let stand for 10 minutes, covered.

3. Add rice mixture to beef; add salt and pepper and mix well.

4. Cut apples into eight equal segments to about 1/2 inch from the bottom; remove cores. (There is an apple slicer-corer on the market that will do this easily in one step.)

5. Open apples slightly and stuff center cavity with meat-rice filling. Push filling in between slices and squeeze apple slices together around filling. Any leftover filling may be shaped into little balls and arranged over and between the apples.

6. Place in a 9x13-inch baking dish; add water to 1/2-inch depth. Cover and bake at 350 degrees for 30 minutes or until apples are soft but not mushy. Delicious served with yogurt as a sauce. May be served the next day.

Yield: 12 dolmas.

Apples on English

English muffins
Butter
Sliced cheese (American or
    Vermont cheddar)

Apple rings (fresh apples,
    peeled, cored, and
    sliced crosswise)
Bacon strips

1. Toast English muffins and butter them.

2. Top each muffin with a slice of cheese and an apple ring.

3. Sprinkle with a dash of cinnamon.

4. Top each muffin with 2 slices of bacon.

5. Broil until bacon is done. (Bacon may broiled first, if desired.) Good for brunch or a light supper.

FAST APPLE FAVORITE

Stir-Fry

Sliced carrots
Broccoli flowerets
Whole string beans

Strips of chicken, pork,
    or beef, marinated in
    soy sauce
Thin wedges of green apple,
    unpeeled

Stir-fry sliced carrots for a few minutes. Add broccoli flowerets and string beans; cook for 10 minutes or so until tender-crisp. Push aside in wok or pan. Add meat strips. Cook and stir; add apple wedges. Continue to cook until meat is done. Stir, cook for 1 minute, and serve, with or without rice.

Cheese Apple Crêpes

Crêpes:
1-1/4 cups flour
3 eggs
1-1/2 cups milk
1/4 cup sugar
1-1/2 teaspoons cinnamon
2 tablespoons butter
Pinch of salt
Butter to cook crêpes

Filling:
1/2 cup sour cream
1/2 cup grated sharp
   cheddar cheese
1 pound tart apples, finely
   chopped
Sugar to taste
Grated sharp cheddar
   cheese for topping
   (about 1/2 cup)

1. For Crêpes: Combine ingredients in a bowl. Beat with mixer until well blended. Let batter stand for at least 1 hour in the refrigerator.

2. For Filling: Combine sour cream and 1/2 cup grated cheese; mix well. Stir in apples. Sweeten with sugar to taste.

3. Butter a 6-inch skillet. Place on medium heat. When water sprinkled on the surface sizzles, the pan is ready. Pour 1/4 cup of crêpe batter into the pan; tilt until the entire surface is covered. Return pan to heat. When batter no longer bubbles, place about 1/3 cup of filling in center. Fold sides over filling.

4. Remove crêpe from pan and place on a baking sheet. Repeat with remaining batter and filling.

5. Sprinkle grated cheese over each crêpe. Bake at 325 degrees until cheese melts.

Yield: About 20 crêpes.

Note: Batter and filling store well, so individual crêpes can be made as needed. Refrigerate unused batter and filling.

Apple Cheese Soufflé

3 apples, finely diced
1 onion, finely diced
4 tablespoons butter
1 clove garlic, crushed, or
    1/4 teaspoon garlic
    powder
1/4 teaspoon each thyme,
    marjoram, and pepper
1/4 cup flour
1 teaspoon salt

1 cup warm milk
1 tablespoon sherry
    (optional)
1 cup grated cheddar cheese
1/4 cup walnuts, finely
    chopped
4 egg yolks
6 egg whites
1/4 teaspoon cream of tartar

1. Preheat oven to 375 degrees.

2. Sauté apples and onion in butter with the garlic and spices until soft. Stir in flour and salt and cook over low heat for a few minutes. Add milk and sherry. Beat with a wire whisk until the sauce is creamy and smooth. Remove from heat. Add cheese and walnuts.

3. Prepare a 6-cup soufflé dish or a deep casserole dish by buttering it and lightly dusting it with bread crumbs or flour. Beat egg yolks and add to the apple mixture. Beat the egg whites and cream of tartar until stiff but not dry. Fold into mixture.

4. Pour into the prepared dish. Reduce oven temperature to 350 degrees. Bake for 45 to 50 minutes. Serve immediately.

Yield: 4 to 6 servings.

All apples, regardless of variety, have ten seeds.

Apple Pancake

2-1/2 tablespoons flour
1/4 teaspoon salt
1/2 cup milk
2 eggs, beaten
4 teaspoons sugar
Grated rind of 1 lemon
2 apples, thinly sliced
3 tablespoons butter
Confectioners' sugar
 (optional)

1. Combine flour, salt, and milk in a mixing bowl and mix to a thin, smooth batter. Add eggs, sugar, and lemon rind; beat well. Add apples; stir into batter.

2. Melt butter in an 8-inch frying pan. Pour apple mixture into the pan, distributing apples evenly over bottom. Cook over medium heat until set and golden brown on the underside.

3. Invert pancake onto a plate the same size as the pan. Add a little more butter to the pan if needed and slide pancake back in to brown the other side.

4. Turn out onto a heated serving dish; serve hot. To make this a dessert, sprinkle the pancake with confectioners' sugar.

Yield: 2 to 4 servings.

Apples are the last fruit to be harvested in the fall.

Notes

Notes

APPLE SIDE DISHES

Vegetables
Salads
Stuffings
Condiments

Baked Stuffed Acorn Squash

3 acorn or Des Moines
   squash
3 apples, unpeeled
3/4 cup nut meats (optional)
1/4 cup melted butter
1/2 cup maple syrup or
   honey

1. Cut squash in halves; scoop out seeds. Dice apples; combine with nuts.

2. Divide apple-nut mixture among the six squash halves; drizzle butter and syrup over each.

3. Place in a baking pan; pour in hot water to 1/2-inch depth. Cover pan loosely with foil. Bake at 400 degrees for 45 minutes or until squash is tender.

Yield: 6 servings.

Isaac Newton discovered the law of gravity in 1666.
The story that the idea came to him while he
was watching an apple fall from the tree
is a myth.

New England Autumn Casserole

2-1/2 cups sliced pumpkin
    or winter squash, peeled
    and seeded
1-1/2 cups sliced apples
1/4 cup butter, melted
3 to 4 tablespoons brown
    sugar
1 teaspoon cinnamon
1/2 cup walnuts or almonds,
    broken up
Salt to taste
Butter

1. Place a layer of pumpkin, then a layer of apples in a 2-quart casserole. (The pumpkin or squash will not cook as quickly, so slice it more thinly than the apples.)

2. Combine 1/4 cup melted butter, sugar, cinnamon, nuts, and salt; drizzle some over apples and pumpkin. Continue alternating layers and drizzling with butter-and-sugar mixture until all ingredients have been used. Dot with a bit more butter.

3. Cover casserole and bake at 350 degrees for 45 to 60 minutes or until pumpkin and apples are tender.

Yield: 4 servings.

One pound of apples is equal to about 3 medium apples,
and yields about 3 cups of sliced apples.

Sweet Apple Cabbage

1 pound red cabbage,
    shredded
2 cups chopped apples
1/3 cup melted butter
2 tablespoons sugar
2 teaspoons salt
1 teaspoon cinnamon

1. In a large pot, toss together all ingredients. Cook over low heat, stirring occasionally, until tender, about 15 to 20 minutes. Add a little water during cooking, if necessary.

2. Serve immediately as a side dish for pork, poultry, or beef.

Yield: About 8 servings.

About the only part of the apple growing that hasn't changed through the ages is the apple-picking . . . and that hasn't changed since Adam and Eve.
John N. Ravage, Vermont Life

Sweet-Potato Scallop

1/2 cup bread crumbs or
    crushed cornflakes
3 tablespoons butter, melted
1/3 cup brown sugar
1 teaspoon salt
1/4 teaspoon cinnamon
1/4 teaspoon nutmeg
1-1/2 cups thinly sliced
    sweet potatoes
1-1/2 cups chopped apples
1 teaspoon lemon juice
3 tablespoons water

1. Stir bread crumbs into butter; add sugar, salt, and spices. Place half the mixture into a greased casserole. Add half the sweet potatoes, then half the apples.

2. Combine lemon juice with water; sprinkle half over apples and potatoes. Repeat sweet potato and apple layers, and top with remaining crumb mixture. Cover; bake at 350 degrees for 45 minutes.

3. Uncover and brown lightly.

Yield: 6 servings.

An apple placed in a bag of potatoes
helps keep them from sprouting.

Jenny's Jellied Apple Salad

3 cups apple juice
2 (3-ounce) packages lemon
    gelatin
1 (20-ounce) can pineapple
    chunks
2 apples, thinly sliced

1. Heat 2 cups of apple juice to boiling. Add gelatin, stir to dissolve over low heat, about 2 minutes.

2. Drain pineapple chunks, reserving liquid; add 1/2 cup of the pineapple juice and remaining 1 cup apple juice to the gelatin mixture. Stir well and chill until slightly jelled, in a 6-cup ring mold or other mold or bowl.

3. Leave the skins on some of the apple slices if desired. Arrange in a pattern in the bottom of the gelatin mixture; add pineapple chunks. Chill until mixture is well set.

4. Turn out gelatin mold and garnish with fresh lettuce leaves, apple wedges, and fresh whole strawberries, if available. Serve with a creamy dressing.

Yield: 8 to 10 servings.

Note: *This salad can also made by substituting 2 envelopes of unflavored gelatin for the lemon gelatin. Either way is good; the lemon is a little tangier.*

Apples consist of 85% water.

Apple-Cider Salad

2 envelopes unflavored
    gelatin
3-1/2 cups apple juice or
    cider
2 tablespoons sugar
Dash of salt
2 apples
1/2 cup chopped carrots
1/2 cup chopped celery

1. Combine gelatin with 1/2 cup of the apple juice, sugar, and salt in a saucepan; stir over low heat until gelatin is dissolved. Add remaining 3 cups apple juice and chill in the refrigerator until partially set, but not firm.

2. Pour about 1 cup of the gelatin mixture into a 6-cup mold. Arrange slices of one apple on top and cover with a layer of gelatin. Combine the other apple, chopped, with carrots and celery; combine with the remaining gelatin mixture and pour into mold. Chill until set.

3. Unmold and serve with lettuce and dressing as desired.

Yield: 8 or more servings.

---

*Apple trees need 30 to 60 days of chill weather
to shed their leaves and take a winter siesta.*

Apple Soufflé Salad

1 (3-ounce) package lemon
  gelatin
1 cup boiling water
3/4 cup cold water
3 tablespoons lemon juice
1/2 teaspoon salt
1/4 cup mayonnaise
2 apples, diced
1/2 cup celery, sliced
1/2 cup seedless grapes
1/4 cup chopped walnuts
Frosted grapes and apple
  slices (garnish; see
  below)

1. Dissolve gelatin in boiling water. Add cold water, lemon juice, salt, and mayonnaise; blend well with a rotary beater. Pour into an ice-cube tray and chill in the freezer for 15 to 20 minutes.

2. Turn the partly frozen mixture into a bowl and whip until light and fluffy. Fold in apples, celery, grapes, and walnuts; pour into a 1-quart mold or 6 individual molds. Chill until firm.

3. To prepare frosted grapes and apple slices, dip fruit into beaten egg white, roll in sugar, and chill. Use to garnish the salad.

Yield: 6 servings.

Apples were imported from England in 1629 by John Winthrop, colonial governor of Massachusetts.

Apple-Yogurt Molded Salad

1 cup apple juice
1-1/3 cups water
2 envelopes unflavored
    gelatin
1/4 cup sugar (or less)
2 cups chopped apples
2 tablespoons lemon juice
1/4 teaspoon salt
1/2 cup chopped nuts
    (optional)
3/4 cup apple yogurt

1. Combine apple juice and water in a saucepan; sprinkle gelatin over juice and stir over low heat until dissolved.

2. Add sugar, apples, lemon juice, salt, and nuts. Chill in the refrigerator until partially set.

3. Fold in yogurt; pour into a 6-cup mold and chill until firmly set. May be served on lettuce leaves as a salad, or topped with whipped cream as a dessert.

Yield: 8 servings.

You can preserve the fresh color of apples by dipping the cut fruit into a mixture of citrus juice and water. Or you can use a commercial ascorbic acid color keeper. Cortland apples will stay white longer than other varieties.

Festive Fruit-Salad Bowl

6 apples, sliced
1 8-ounce can pineapple
   chunks, drained
2 bananas, sliced
1/2 cup finely chopped
   walnuts
3 cups miniature
   marshmallows

Dressing:
1 cup mayonnaise
4 tablespoons milk

1. Mix fruit, nuts, and marshmallows in large bowl.

2. Mix dressing ingredients well with a rotary beater or a wire whisk. Toss dressing with the fruit mixture; chill.

3. Serve on lettuce leaves; or serve plain as a dessert.

Yield: About 8 servings.

The apple's reputation as nature's toothbrush comes from the evidence that eating raw apples "brushes" the teeth, cleanses the mouth of 96.7% of oral bacteria, and exercises the teeth and gums. Dentists claim that the best times to eat an apple are after meals and just before going to bed.

Frosty Apple Salad

2 (3-ounce) packages cream
    cheese, softened
1 (8-ounce) can crushed
    pineapple, undrained
2 tablespoons syrup from
    maraschino cherries
1/4 cup chopped maraschino
    cherries
1-1/2 cups chopped apples,
    unpeeled
1/2 cup sour cream

1. Mix cream cheese, pineapple, and cherry syrup. Process in a blender for a few seconds, or cream together well with a fork.

2. Add chopped cherries and apples; fold in sour cream. Freeze in an ice-cube tray until firm. Cut into squares and serve on lettuce leaves.

Yield: About 8 servings.

"Very astonishing indeed! Strange thing!
(Turning the Dumpling round, rejoiced the King). . . .
"But, Goody, tell me where, where, where's the Seam?"
"Sire there's no Seam," Quoth she; "I never knew
That folks did Apple Dumplings sew."
"No!" cried the staring Monarch with a grin;
"How, how the devil got the Apple in?
John Wolcott, The Apple Dumplings and the King

All-Purpose Apple Stuffing

1 cup Italian flavored
  breadcrumbs
1 apple, chopped
1 cup hot water
4 tablespoons olive oil

1. Mix breadcrumbs, apple, hot water, and 2 tablespoons of the oil. Use remaining oil to brush vegetables.

a. To stuff onions: Halve large onions and push out their centers; set onion shells aside. Chop the onion centers, add them to the stuffing mixture, and stuff the onion shells.

b. To stuff mushrooms: Break off stems, chop, and add to the stuffing mixture.

c. To stuff tomatoes: Remove inner part of tomato, chop, add to the stuffing mixture.

d. To stuff zucchini or eggplant: Halve and scoop out center, chop, and add to the stuffing mixture.

e. To stuff poultry and seafood: Use as you would any other stuffing.

2. Bake stuffed vegetables at 350 degrees for about 40 minutes. Bake poultry or seafood according to your usual procedure.

Yield: 2 or more cups of stuffing, depending upon the quantity of added ingredients listed in Steps a. through e.

He kept him as the apple of his eye.
Deuteronomy 32:10

Jiffy Apple Stuffing

2 or 3 medium onions,
    chopped
2 stalks celery, diced
1/2 cup butter
1 (8-ounce) package Herb
    Bread Stuffing
1 cup walnuts, coarsely
    chopped
4 apples, chopped (Macs
    are good)

1. Sauté onions and celery in butter until light brown.

2. Prepare Herb Bread Stuffing according to package directions.

3. Add sautéed onions and celery, walnuts, and apples.

Yield: Stuffing for 6 to 8 pounds of poultry.

The Hebrew word for apple does not appear in the biblical
account of Adam and Eve. Since it is doubtful that
the apple existed in that part of the world at that
time it is believed that the forbidden fruit
may have been the apricot, which was
plentiful in the Holy Land.

Honey-Mustard Dressing

1/4 cup honey
1/2 cup applesauce
1 teaspoon spicy mustard
1/4 cup lemon juice
1 teaspoon grated lemon peel
3 tablespoons vinegar
1/2 cup vegetable oil
Salt and pepper to taste

1. Mix all ingredients together well with a rotary beater or a wire whisk.

2. Adjust seasonings. Chill.

3. Shake and serve with fresh mixed greens, orange and grapefruit segments, or fruit salad of your choice.

Yield: About 1-1/2 cups dressing.

Since apples keep longer than most other fruits, it is often economical to buy them in large amounts. They should be stored either in a cool, well-ventilated cellar or on a sheltered back porch. The cooler the storage area the better, although the temperature should not go below freezing. Store only good apples, as one bad one will spoil the entire lot.

Tomato Chutney

4 pounds ripe tomatoes,
  cored and chopped
1 pound apples, chopped
3 onions, finely chopped
2 cups vinegar
2 tablespoons salt
2 cups brown sugar
1 cup seedless raisins
1 teaspoon dry mustard
1/2 teaspoon cayenne pepper

1. Mix all ingredients and cook, stirring occasionally, for about 1-1/2 hours, or until thick and clear.

2. Pour into hot, sterilized pint jars, leaving 1/2-inch headspace. Add lids and tighten screw bands. Process in boiling water canner. Fill canner halfway with water and preheat to 180 degrees. Load sealed jars onto the canner rack and lower with handles, or load one jar at a time with jar lifter onto rack in canner. Add water if needed to a level of one inch above jars; cover. When water boils vigorously, lower heat to maintain a gentle boil.

3. Process half-pints and pints for 5 minutes. (For altitudes over 1000 feet, process for 10 minutes; for altitudes over 6000 feet, process for 15 minutes.)

4. Let jars cool for up to 24 hours. Remove screw bands and check lid seals to be sure center of lid is indented. Store in a cool, dark place.

Yield: About 5 pints.

---

*Apple: the earth, the globe; any large town or city;
a street or district in which excitement
or activity may be found.*

Indian Relish

12 green tomatoes
12 tart apples
3 onions
5 cups white vinegar
5 cups sugar
1 teaspoon red pepper
3 teaspoons ginger
1 teaspoon turmeric
1 teaspoon salt

1. Chop the tomatoes, apples, and onions; put them into a large strainer or colander and drain off about 2 cups liquid. Discard the liquid.

2. Meanwhile, heat the vinegar, sugar, spices, and salt together in a large saucepan. Cook until liquid boils vigorously. Remove from heat; add the chopped mixture. Return to a boil. Reduce heat and cook slowly for 10 minutes, stirring frequently.

3. Pour into hot, sterilized pint jars leaving 1/2-inch headspace. Add lids and tighten screw bands. Process in boiling water canner. Fill canner halfway with water and preheat to 180 degrees. Load sealed jars onto the canner rack and lower with handles, or load one jar at a time with jar lifter onto rack in canner. Add water if needed to a level of one inch above jars; cover. When water boils vigorously, lower heat to maintain a gentle boil.

4. Process half-pints and pints for 10 minutes. (For altitudes over 1000 feet, process for 15 minutes; for altitudes over 6000 feet, process for 20 minutes.)

5. Let jars cool for up to 24 hours. Remove screw bands and check lid seals to be sure center of lid is indented. Store in a cool, dark place.

Yield: About 8 pints.

Rosy Applesauce

5 to 6 pounds (15 to 20)
  red-skinned apples
1 cup water
1 cup sugar
1/2 cup light brown sugar
1 teaspoon cinnamon
  (optional)

1. Wash apples; remove bud and stem areas. Do not peel or core. Cut into quarters.

2. Place apples into a 5-quart saucepan with water; bring to a boil, and simmer for 30 to 40 minutes or until the pulp softens and separates from the peel. Stir occasionally.

4. Press through a food mill or a colander.

5. Add sugar and cinnamon to the warm applesauce and allow to stand until cool enough to eat. Serve warm or chilled.

Yield: 6 to 8 cups thick, rosy-colored applesauce.

Most apples are marketed by grade, which is determined according to their color, maturity, lack of defects, and general appearance. The US grades for apples are US Extra Fancy, US Fancy, US No. 1, and combinations of these grades. US No. 2 is a less desirable grade, but fine for cooking purposes.

Vermont Apple Butter

4 pounds (about 12) apples, cored and cut into eighths
1/2 cup water or cider
2 cups sugar
1 teaspoon grated lemon peel
1/4 teaspoon cinnamon
1/4 teaspoon cloves
1/4 teaspoon allspice
1/4 teaspoon salt
1/8 teaspoon nutmeg (optional)

1. Cook apples in water over low heat for about 45 minutes or until tender and mushy.

2. Put apples through a food mill or a colander. Add sugar, lemon peel, spices, and salt; cook until thick and glossy for about 30 minutes, stirring frequently.

3. Pour into hot, sterilized half-pint jars, leaving 1/4-inch headspace. Add lids and tighten screw bands. Process in boiling water canner. Fill canner halfway with water and preheat to 180 degrees. Load sealed jars onto the canner rack and lower with handles, or load one jar at a time with jar lifter onto rack in canner. Add water if needed to a level of one inch above jars; cover. When water boils vigorously, lower heat to maintain a gentle boil.

4. Process half-pints or pints for 5 minutes. (For altitudes over 3000 feet, process for 10 minutes; for altitudes over 6000 feet, process for 15 minutes.)

5. Let jars cool for up to 24 hours. Remove screw bands and check lid seals to be sure center of lid is indented. Store in a cool, dark place.

Yield: 4 half-pint jars.

Apple Jelly

3 pounds (about 9) apples*
3 cups water
3 cups sugar

2 tablespoons lemon juice,
or 1/2 teaspoon
peppermint extract
(optional)

1. Remove stem and blossom ends of apples, but do not core or peel. Cut apples into small chunks and put into a kettle with water. Cover and bring to a boil over high heat; lower heat and simmer for about 20 minutes or until apples are very tender.

2. Turn cooked fruit and juice into a jelly bag or several thicknesses of dampened cheesecloth; let juice drain into a kettle, shifting pulp occasionally to keep the juice flowing.

3. Combine 4 cups of the apple juice in the kettle with sugar, and lemon juice or peppermint extract. Boil rapidly until mixture is 8 degrees above the boiling point of water, or until the jelly sheets from a spoon. Skim foam off jelly.

4. Pour into hot, sterilized half-pint jars, leaving 1/4-inch headspace. Add lids and tighten screw bands. Process in boiling water canner. Fill canner halfway with water and preheat to 180 degrees. Load sealed jars onto the canner rack and lower with handles, or load one jar at a time with jar lifter onto rack in canner. Add water if needed to a level of one inch above jars; cover. When water boils vigorously, lower heat to maintain a gentle boil.

5. Process half-pints or pints for 5 minutes. (For altitudes over 1000 feet, process for 10 minutes; for altitudes over 6000 feet, process for 15 minutes.)

6. Let jars cool for up to 24 hours. Remove screw bands and check lid seals to be sure center of lid is indented. Store in a cool, dark place.

Yield: About 4 half-pint jars.

*Use slightly underripe apples, or at least one quarter underripe and three quarters ripe.

Notes

Notes

APPLE BREADS

Yeast Breads
Coffeecakes
Doughnuts
Muffins

Apple Raisin Braid

Dough:
1 package dry yeast
1/4 cup warm water
1/4 cup sugar
1/2 cup milk
1/4 cup butter
1 egg
1 cup grated apples
3 cups flour
1/2 teaspoon salt

Filling:
1/2 cup sugar
2 tablespoons flour
1/2 cup water
1 tablespoon lemon juice
1-1/2 cups raisins
2 cups chopped apples

Icing:
1 tablespoon melted butter
1 tablespoon milk
Confectioners' sugar

1. **For Dough:** Mix yeast and warm water; add sugar. Scald milk; add butter. Add milk mixture and egg to yeast; stir in apples, flour, and salt. Knead until well blended; let rise until doubled.

2. **For Filling:** While dough is rising, mix sugar and flour; add water and lemon juice; mix in raisins. Heat until thick and raisins are soft. Add apples.

3. Knead dough again and divide into two parts. Roll or flatten to a long rectangle about 1/2 inch thick on a lightly greased cookie sheet. At 1-inch intervals along the sides, slit dough one third of the width, leaving the center uncut. Spread the center with half of the filling.

4. Braid by bringing side strips over the filling from alternate sides, crossing them in the middle. Repeat with the other half of the dough. Let rise until doubled.

5. Bake at 375 degrees for 30 minutes or until golden brown.

6. **For Icing:** Combine melted butter and milk; add confectioners' sugar until of spreading consistency. Use as a glaze for the top of the bread.

Yield: 2 braids.

Apple Honey-Buns

1/2 cup butter
1 cup brown sugar
1 teaspoon cinnamon
1 tablespoon honey
1/3 cup milk
1 (16-ounce) package
    Hot Roll Mix
3/4 cup very warm water
1/3 cup sugar
1 egg
1/2 cup chopped nuts
1-1/2 cups chopped apples

1. Combine butter, brown sugar, cinnamon, honey, and milk in a small saucepan. Stir over low heat until butter melts and mixture is smooth. Pour half of the mixture into an ungreased 13x9x2-inch baking pan; reserve the remaining mixture.

2. Dissolve the yeast from the Hot Roll Mix in warm water in a large bowl; stir in sugar, egg, and nuts. Add flour mixture from Hot Roll Mix and apples; blend well.

3. Drop dough by heaping tablespoonfuls on top of the brown sugar mixture in the pan, forming 15 rolls. Drizzle with remaining brown sugar mixture.

4. Cover; let rise in a warm place for 45 to 60 minutes or until light and doubled in bulk.

5. Bake for 30 to 35 minutes or until golden. Let stand a few minutes; remove from pan.

Yield: 15 honey-buns.

Sweet Apple Bread

Bread:
2 loaves frozen Bread Dough
2 tablespoons butter
2 cups diced apples
3/4 cup light brown sugar
2 teaspoons cinnamon
1/2 cup raisins

Glaze:
1-1/2 cups confectioners'
  sugar
2 tablespoons milk
1/2 teaspoon lemon juice
1/4 teaspoon cinnamon
  (optional)
1/2 cup chopped nuts
  (garnish)

1. Place Bread Dough in a lightly greased large bowl; let rise until doubled in size.

2. Roll out dough into a rectangle about 1/2 inch thick. Spread with butter; sprinkle with apples, brown sugar, cinnamon, and raisins.

3. Roll up like a jelly roll; place seam side down in a large (10-inch) tube pan. Wet the two ends of the roll with water and pinch together to seal.

4. Let rise in a warm place until doubled in size. Bake at 375 degrees for about 35 minutes or until golden brown. Cool on a wire rack.

5. For Glaze: Blend confectioners' sugar, milk, lemon juice, and cinnamon together until smooth. Remove bread from pan and spread with glaze. Sprinkle with nuts.

Yield: 1 bread ring.

Buttery Apple Flake Loaf

1/3 cup butter
4 apples, diced
1/2 teaspoon cinnamon
1 cup crushed macaroon
    cookies
2 (8-ounce) packages
    refrigerated Quick
    Butterflake Dinner Rolls
3 tablespoons crushed sugar
    cubes

1. Melt 4 tablespoons of the butter in a skillet; add apples and cinnamon, turning frequently, until golden. Fold in crushed macaroons, mixing well.

2. Halve rolls and put them together again with 1 tablespoon of the apple mixture for each. Stand the rolls on edge in a lightly buttered 9x5x3-inch glass loaf pan, making two rows.

3. Spoon the remaining filling in between the rolls. Drizzle the loaf with the remaining butter, melted. Sprinkle with coarse crystal sugar.

4. Bake at 350 degrees for 30 to 35 minutes. Loosen edges; turn out of pan immediately. Serve warm.

Yield: 1 loaf.

*The crab apple is parent to all apple varieties
that are now growing.*

Raisin Spice Oatmeal Bread

1-1/2 cups flour
1 teaspoon baking powder
1 teaspoon baking soda
1-1/2 teaspoons salt
1 teaspoon cinnamon
1/2 teaspoon nutmeg
2/3 cup brown sugar
2 eggs, beaten
1 cup applesauce
1 cup quick or old-fashioned
    oats, uncooked
1 cup raisins
1/3 cup vegetable oil or
    melted butter

1. Sift together flour, baking powder, baking soda, salt, and spices. Add brown sugar, eggs, and applesauce; beat until well blended. Stir in oats, raisins, and oil.

2. Fill a buttered 9x5-inch loaf pan. Bake at 350 degrees for about 1 hour.

3. Remove from pan immediately; cool. For ease in slicing, wrap cooled bread and store for one day.

Yield: 1 loaf.

Late-maturing apples picked after the first frost are juicier, crispier, and contain more fruit sugar than apples picked earlier in the season.

Quick Raisin Bran Bread

2 cups raisin bran cereal
1-1/2 cups applesauce
1/3 cup sugar
1/2 cup butter, melted
2 eggs, well beaten
1-1/2 cups whole wheat flour
1 tablespoon baking powder
1/4 teaspoon salt

1. Combine cereal and applesauce in a mixing bowl and let stand until cereal is moistened.

2. Add sugar and melted butter, mixing well; stir in eggs.

3. Add sifted dry ingredients, stirring only until combined. Pour into a buttered 9x5-inch loaf pan. Bake at 350 degrees for about 1 hour or until bread tests done. Cool and remove from pan.

Yield: One 9x5-inch loaf.

Note: This recipe also makes excellent muffins. Bake medium-sized muffins for about 30 minutes. Chopped nuts or cranberries or both may be added—about 3/4 cup of each.

Apple Cheese Bread

1/2 cup butter
1/3 cup sugar
1/3 cup honey
2 eggs
1 cup whole wheat flour
1 cup unbleached white flour
1 teaspoon baking powder
1/2 teaspoon baking soda
1/2 teaspoon salt
1-1/2 cups grated apples
1/2 cup grated sharp
    cheddar cheese
1/2 cup chopped waluuts

1. Cream together butter and sugar. Mix in honey and eggs. Sift together dry ingredients and add to creamed mixture. Fold in apples, cheddar cheese, and nuts.

2. Spoon batter into a buttered 9x5-inch loaf pan. Bake at 350 degrees for 50 to 60 minutes. Remove from pan and cool thoroughly. Tastes best the next day.

Yield: 1 loaf.

The average American consumes close to 40 pounds of apples a year. Nearly half are eaten fresh.

Apple Cornbread

1-1/4 cups cornmeal
1-3/4 cups flour
2/3 cup sugar
4 teaspoons baking powder
1/2 teaspoon salt
2 eggs, beaten
1-1/2 cups milk
2 tablespoons butter,
    softened
3 apples, sliced
1/3 cup brown sugar
1 tablespoon flour
1 tablespoon butter
1/2 teaspoon cinnamon

1. Sift together the first 5 ingredients. Mix in eggs and milk combined with 2 tablespoons melted butter.

2. Pour batter into a buttered 13x9-inch pan. Arrange apple slices up and down batter in rows.

3. Combine remaining ingredients and sprinkle over apples. Bake at 425 degrees (400 degrees if you are using a glass pan) for 25 minutes until browned.

Yield: About 2 dozen squares.

Apple Coffeecake

1/3 cup butter
1 cup sugar
2 eggs
1 teaspoon vanilla
1-1/2 cups flour
2 teaspoons baking powder
1/2 teaspoon nutmeg
1/4 teaspoon salt
2/3 cup milk
4 apples, finely chopped
1 tablespoon cinnamon
1 tablespoon sugar
1/2 cup chopped walnuts

1. Cream together butter and sugar until fluffy. Add eggs and vanilla; beat well. Sift together dry ingredients. Add to creamed mixture alternately with milk, beating smooth after each addition. Fold in apples. Pour into a buttered 9-inch square pan.

2. Combine remaining ingredients and sprinkle over batter. Bake at 375 degrees for 25 to 30 minutes.

Yield: 1 coffeecake.

Note: The batter for this cake may be prepared the night before and kept in the refrigerator until ready to bake.

He that is won with a nut may be lost with an apple.
Thomas Fuller, Gnomologia No. 2201

Aunt Rashe's Streusel Coffeecake

Streusel:
1/2 cup brown sugar
2 tablespoons flour
1 teaspoon cinnamon
2 tablespoons softened butter
1/2 cup chopped nuts

Batter:
1-1/2 cups flour
1 tablespoon baking powder
1/2 teaspoon salt
3/4 cup sugar
1/4 cup butter
1/2 cup milk
1 egg
1-1/2 cups apples, sliced

1. For Streusel: Combine ingredients and set aside.

2. For Batter: Sift together flour, baking powder, salt, and sugar.

3. Cut in butter with a pastry blender or two knives.

4. Mix in egg and milk.

5. Pour half of the batter into a greased 9-inch square cake pan. Arrange the apple slices over the batter and sprinkle with half of the streusel. Add the remaining batter and top with the remaining streusel.

6. Bake at 350 degrees for 35 minutes or until golden brown.

Yield: One 9-inch coffeecake.

Baked Apple Coconut Doughnuts

Doughnuts:
2-1/2 cups flour
2-1/2 teaspoons baking
    powder
1/2 teaspoon salt
1/2 teaspoon nutmeg
1/2 cup sugar
2/3 cup butter
1 cup milk
1 egg, well beaten
1 cup grated apple
1/2 cup shredded coconut

Topping:
1/3 cup melted butter
1/3 cup sugar
1 teaspoon cinnamon

1. Sift together flour, baking powder, salt, nutmeg, and sugar. Cut in the butter until mixture resembles fine crumbs.

2. Mix together milk, egg, apple, and coconut; add all at once to flour mixture and mix quickly and thoroughly.

3. Fill buttered large muffin tins two-thirds full. Bake at 350 degrees for 25 minutes or until golden brown.

4. Remove from pan. Immediately dunk doughnut tops in melted butter and then in combined sugar and cinnamon.

Yield: About 18 doughnuts.

Unripe or hard apples should be held at a cool 60 to 70 degrees room temperature until ready to eat.

Old-Fashioned Doughnut Balls

2 eggs
1 cup sugar
1 teaspoon salt
1 teaspoon nutmeg
1/2 teaspoon cinnamon
1/4 cup butter, softened
1 cup buttermilk
3-3/4 cups flour
1 teaspoon baking powder
1 teaspoon baking soda
1 cup grated apple
Fat or oil for deep frying
Cinnamon and sugar

1. Beat eggs, sugar, salt, spices, and shortening together well. Add buttermilk.

2. Combine flour, baking powder, and baking soda and stir into batter; add grated apple. Let set in refrigerator while fat heats.

3. Heat fat to about 370 degrees. Drop batter by teaspoonfuls into the hot fat, turning once. Roll doughnut balls in a mixture of cinnamon and sugar while still slightly warm.

Yield: 5 dozen doughnut balls.

*Controlled Atmosphere Storage (CA Storage) allows
apples to be eaten year-round. The process slows
down the rate of respiration and the apple
continues to "live" for up to
ten months.*

Apple Muffins

3/4 cup milk
1 egg, beaten
1/4 cup melted butter
2 cups unsifted flour
1/2 cup sugar
1 tablespoon baking powder
1/2 teaspoon salt
1 teaspoon cinnamon
    (optional)
1 cup finely chopped apples
1/2 cup raisins

1. Add milk to egg; stir in butter.

2. Mix dry ingredients thoroughly; stir in apples and raisins.

3. Add milk and egg mixture to dry ingredients and stir just until moistened. Do not overmix; batter should be lumpy.

4. Fill greased muffin tins two-thirds full. Bake at 400 degrees for 20 to 25 minutes or until golden brown.

Yield: 12 muffins.

Apples have flourished in Britain ever since Caesar's Roman legions invaded those isles.

Notes

APPLE PASTRIES

Pies
Cakes
Tortes
Strudels

Apple Cheese Pie

Pie:
3/4 cup sugar
2 tablespoons flour
1/4 teaspoon salt
1 cup small-curd cottage
cheese
2 eggs
1 tablespoon lemon juice
1 teaspoon vanilla
2-1/2 cups chopped apples
9-inch pie shell (graham
cracker or pastry)

Topping:
1/3 cup flour
1/4 cup sugar
1 teaspoon cinnamon
4 tablespoons butter

1. For Pie: Combine sugar, flour, and salt. Blend in cottage cheese, eggs, lemon juice, and vanilla; mix thoroughly. Stir in apples. Spoon into pie shell.

2. For Topping: Sift together flour, sugar, and cinnamon. Cut in butter until mixture is crumbly; sprinkle over pie. Bake at 375 degrees for 40 to 50 minutes.

Yield: One 9-inch pie.

Apple pie without cheese
Is like a kiss without a squeeze.
Unknown

Apple Custard Cream Pie

Pie:
9-inch pie shell, fluted high
1 tablespoon flour
8 apples, quartered
1 cup sugar
1 teaspoon cinnamon
Dash of nutmeg
1 tablespoon butter

Custard:
1 small egg
1/2 cup light cream
1/4 cup sugar
1 teaspoon vanilla

1. For Pie: Dust bottom of pie shell with flour. Arrange apples in pie shell; sprinkle with sugar combined with cinnamon and nutmeg. Dot with butter.

2. Cover tightly with foil and bake at 425 degrees for about 30 minutes or until apples are cooked through.

3. For Custard: While pie is baking, combine custard ingredients and beat well.

4. Remove pie from oven and pour custard evenly over apples in pie shell.

5. Lower oven temperature to 325 degrees and bake for 35 minutes longer.

Yield: One 9-inch pie.

Storing apples in a plastic bag in the refrigerator helps to maintain proper humidity.

Caramel Apple Pie

Pie:
5-1/2 cups sliced apples
1/4 cup water
9-inch pie shell
3/4 cup graham cracker
    crumbs
3/4 cup sugar
1 tablespoon flour
1/2 teaspoon cinnamon
1/2 teaspoon nutmeg
1/4 teaspoon salt
1/2 cup pecans, chopped
1/3 cup butter, melted

Sauce:
8 ounces caramels
1/2 cup hot milk

1. **For Pie:** Cook apple slices in water for 3 minutes. Cool.

2. Arrange apple slices in pie shell. Mix graham cracker crumbs, sugar, flour, cinnamon, nutmeg, salt, pecans, and melted butter. Sprinkle over apples.

3. Bake at 425 degrees for 10 minutes; reduce heat to 350 degrees and continue baking for 20 minutes longer.

4. **For Sauce:** Meanwhile, combine caramels and milk in the top of a double boiler; cook over hot water until smooth.

5. Pour caramel sauce over the top of the hot pie. Reduce heat to 250 degrees and continue baking for 10 minutes longer.

Yield: One 9-inch pie.

Note: The pie will be easier to slice if allowed to cool until caramel has set slightly.

Apple Praline Pie

5 cups sliced apples
1/2 cup sugar
2 tablespoons quick-cooking
    tapioca
1-1/2 teaspoons lemon juice
1/2 cup flour
1/4 cup dark brown sugar
1/2 cup chopped pecans
1/4 cup butter
9-inch pie shell

1. Combine apples, sugar, tapioca, and lemon juice in a large bowl; let stand for 15 minutes.

2. Combine remaining ingredients, except pie shell, cutting in butter until crumbs form.

3. Sprinkle one third of the crumb mixture into the bottom of the pie shell. Cover with the apple mixture; sprinkle remaining crumbs on top.

4. Bake at 450 degrees for 10 minutes. Reduce heat to 350 degrees and continue baking for about 25 minutes longer or until nicely browned.

Yield: One 9-inch pie.

---

*Apple pie was a part of English cookery at least two
centuries before the settling of America.
The English version is made with
a puff paste.*

Cranberry-Glazed Cheese Pie

Crust:
1-1/2 cups graham cracker
    or cookie crumbs
3 tablespoons sugar
1/3 cup butter, melted

Filling:
1 (3-ounce) package lemon
    gelatin
1-1/4 cups boiling water
1 (8-ounce) package cream
    cheese, softened
1-1/2 cups grated apple
1 tablespoon sugar

Topping:
2 teaspoons cornstarch
1 tablespoon sugar
1/2 cup cranberry or
    cranapple juice
1 apple, thinly sliced

1. For Crust: Combine crumbs, sugar, and butter; mix well. Press into a 9-inch pie plate. Bake at 350 degrees for 10 minutes. Cool.

2. For Filling: Dissolve gelatin in boiling water; add cream cheese and blend until well mixed. Refrigerate until slightly jelled. Beat again. Mix grated apple with sugar; add to gelatin mixture, blend, and pour into prepared crust. Chill.

3. For Topping: Mix cornstarch and sugar; add juice and heat, stirring until thickened. Add apple slices and cook until soft. Arrange slices on top of pie, pouring any remaining juice mixture over. Chill.

Yield: One 9-inch pie.

Grated Apple Meringue Pie

4 large apples, grated
1/2 cup sugar
1 cup milk
2 tablespoons melted butter
3 eggs (reserve 2 whites for
    meringue)
1/2 cup raisins
1/2 teaspoon nutmeg
9-inch pie shell
1/4 cup confectioners' sugar
1/4 cup currant or other
    fruit jelly

1. Combine grated apples with sugar, milk, melted butter, one whole egg, and two egg yolks; blend well. Add raisins and nutmeg and pour into pie shell.

2. Bake at 350 degrees for about 40 minutes or until a knife inserted in the custard comes out clean. Cool.

3. Make meringue: beat the two reserved egg whites until soft peaks form; add confectioners' sugar gradually and continue beating until quite stiff.

4. Spread the cooled pie first with jelly and then with meringue. Bake at 350 degrees for about 10 minutes or until lightly browned.

Yield: One 9-inch pie.

Note: This pie is also good if made without the jelly, but in that case a little more sugar may be needed in the pie.

Honey of an Apple Pie

Pastry:
2 cups flour
1 teaspoon salt
1/3 cup shortening
1/3 cup butter
4 to 5 tablespoons cold water

Filling:
6 cooking apples, sliced
2 tablespoons flour
2 teaspoons cinnamon
1/2 cup honey*

1. For Pastry: Place flour and salt in a large bowl; add shortening and butter and cut in until the mixture is in pieces the size of peas. Add water a little at a time until the dough can be patted into two balls. Chill. Roll dough into two circles; line a 10-inch pie plate with one circle, and trim.

2. For Filling: Sprinkle a light film of flour into the prepared pie shell. Place one third of the sliced apples into the pie shell and sprinkle with a bit of flour and cinnamon; repeat twice. Pour honey over all.

3. Cover with the top pastry crust and pierce well; press edges firmly together. Bake at 350 degrees for 50 minutes or until crust is golden brown. Serve with ice cream, if desired.

*Instead of honey, sugar may be used—about 2/3 cup or less, to taste. Sprinkle sugar with flour and cinnamon over the apples as described above.

Yield: One 10-inch pie.

Sour Cream Apple Pie

9-inch pie shell

Topping:
2 tablespoons butter,
   softened
1/4 cup sugar
1 tablespoon flour
1/2 teaspoon cinnamon

Filling:
1 cup sour cream
2 eggs
2 tablespoons flour
1/2 cup sugar
1 teaspoon vanilla
4 large apples

1. For Topping: Combine all ingredients with a fork. Set aside in the refrigerator.

2. For Filling: Combine sour cream, eggs, flour, sugar, and vanilla; mix well. Using the slice side of a grater, slice apples into sour cream mixture and fold in.

3. Pour the filling into the pie shell and smooth top with a spoon. Crumble the topping over the filling. Bake at 350 degrees for 1 hour.

Yield: One 9-inch pie.

Note: Another way to prepare this pie is to arrange the sliced apples in the pie shell and pour the sour cream mixture over them; then proceed as above.

But when I undress me
Each night upon my knees
Will ask the Lord to bless me
With apple pie and cheese!
Eugene Field, Apple Pie and Cheese

Barney's Hot Apple Pie

1-1/2 pounds apples, sliced
1 cup raisins
1 cup sugar
3/4 cup white wine

1 tablespoon cinnamon
1 teaspoon nutmeg
20 thin slices white bread
3/4 cup butter, melted

1. Combine apples, raisins, sugar, wine, cinnamon, and nutmeg. Cook over medium heat for 5 minutes. Stir gently so as not to break the apple slices.

2. Trim the crusts off bread slices. Cut corners off ten of the slices to form each into an octagon shape. Cut each of the remaining ten slices into four squares.

3. Butter five 10-ounce deep pie dishes or ovenproof 5-inch bowls. Dip one face of each octagon in melted butter and place, buttered side down, in the bottom of each dish.

4. Dip corners of bread squares in butter and fit into each dish as follows: squeeze point of one square into octagon on bottom, covering side of dish; repeat with seven more squares, overlapping around dish and completely encircling the inside of the dish. (You will use eight bread squares per bowl.)

5. Fill each dish with apple mixture. Completely soak the remaining five bread octagons in butter and place one on top of each dish, completely sealing in the apple mixture.

6. Place the dishes on a baking sheet and bake at 350 degrees for 45 minutes or until golden brown on the sides as well as on top. Remove from oven and let stand for about 10 minutes.

7. Unmold each pie onto a dinner plate and surround with your favorite vanilla sauce or rum sauce.

Yield: 5 small pies.

Apple Flan

Pastry:
2 cups flour
1/2 cup butter
1/4 cup superfine sugar
2 egg yolks
1/4 teaspoon vanilla
1/4 cup water

Topping:
1/4 cup apricot jam
1 tablespoon prune juice or
water

Filling:
2 pounds cooking apples,
cut in large slices
5/8 cup white wine or apple
juice
Grated rind of 1/2 lemon
4 tablespoons butter
1/2 cup sugar
4 crisp apples, thinly sliced

1. For Pastry: Sift flour into a mixing bowl; make a well, and add butter (cut in small pieces), superfine sugar, egg yolks, vanilla, and water. Blend with fingertips. Knead lightly. Chill for 30 minutes. Roll out to line an 8-inch flan ring or a shallow 8-inch cake pan.

2. For Filling: Place apples in a saucepan with wine or apple juice, lemon rind, butter, and 1/4 cup of the sugar. Cover and simmer gently until apples are tender. Puree cooked apples in a blender and place in the pie shell.

3. Arrange thinly sliced apples on top of the apple puree, overlapping them. Sprinkle with the remaining 1/4 cup sugar. Bake at 375 degrees for 25 to 30 minutes or until golden brown.

4. For Topping: Heat apricot jam with prune juice. Spoon over hot cooked flan. Serve with whipped cream if desired.

Yield: One 8-inch flan.

Rickrack Apple Tart

Pastry:
1/4 cup butter, chilled
1 cup flour
1/2 teaspoon salt
1 tablespoon confectioners'
    sugar
1 egg yolk

Filling:
7 tart cooking apples,
    halved
1/2 cup honey
1/4 cup sugar
2 tablespoons flour
1/2 teaspoon cinnamon
2 tablespoons butter
1/4 cup cream

1. For Pastry: Cut butter into dry ingredients with a pastry blender; stir in egg yolk. With fingertips, press dough over bottom and up on sides of a 9-inch pie plate, making a 1/2-inch standing dough rim. With a pastry wheel, roll a rickrack edge over the pastry along the rim of the shell.

2. For Filling: Slice 4 apple halves thinly into the pie shell in a single layer. Combine honey, sugar, flour, and cinnamon; drizzle half of this mixture over apples. Arrange the remaining apple halves, cut side down, in a single layer on top of the apple slices. Sprinkle with the remaining honey mixture; dot with butter. Slowly pour in cream near the center of the pie.

3. Bake at 400 degrees for 1 hour. Apples will be tender, but retain their shape. Syrupy juices will thicken as pie cools. After taking the pie from the oven, gently press the apples down very lightly into the juices. Serve warm or cold.

Yield: One 9-inch tart.

*The United States produces approximately
one quarter of the world's apple crop.*

Apple Cheese Tarts

1 (3-ounce) package cream
   cheese, softened
1 tablespoon apple cider
1/2 cup heavy cream
2 tablespoons confectioners'
   sugar
1 (1-pound, 2-ounce) package
   Slice'n Bake Sugar
   Cookies
3 apples, thinly sliced

1. Combine cream cheese and apple cider. Whip cream and sugar together until stiff; fold into cream cheese.

2. Bake Sugar Cookies as directed on package. Immediately after removing them from oven, indent the center of each cookie with the back of a tablespoon. Remove from baking sheet; cool.

3. Place apple slices in boiling water for 1 minute. Rinse with cold water.

4. Just before serving, place about 1 teaspoon of cream cheese filling on each cookie. Top each with two apple slices.

Yield: 3-1/2 dozen tarts.

The friendly cow all red and white,
I love with all my heart:
She gives me cream with all her might,
To eat with apple-tart.
Robert Louis Stevenson, A Child's Garden of Verses

Pam's Chocolate Birthday Cake

2-1/2 cups flour
2-1/2 teaspoons baking
    powder
1/2 teaspoon baking soda
1/2 teaspoon salt
3 (1-ounce) squares baking
    chocolate
3/4 cup butter
1-1/2 cups sugar
2 eggs, well beaten
1 cup applesauce
3/4 cup soured milk

1. Sift together dry ingredients and set aside.

2. Melt chocolate and butter in a heavy pan over low heat. Combine with sugar in a mixing bowl; add eggs in thirds, beating thoroughly after each addition.

3. Add dry ingredients alternately with applesauce combined with milk, ending with dry ingredients. Do not overbeat; beat just enough to make mixture smooth.

4. Turn batter into a lightly greased 10-inch tube pan. Bake at 350 degrees for about 1 hour or until a cake tester comes out clean.

Yield: One 10-inch cake.

Notes: To make soured milk, place 2 teaspoons vinegar or lemon juice into a measuring cup. Add fresh milk to make 3/4 cup liquid. Or, in place of soured milk, try buttermilk or plain yogurt. For an even darker chocolate cake, add an additional square of baking chocolate, reducing butter by 1 tablespoon. Sift confectioners' sugar over the cake if you choose not to decorate with frosting.

Aeble Kage (Apple Cake)

3 pounds (about 9) apples,
    cut in small pieces
1/2 cup water
3/4 cup sugar
2 cups bread crumbs
2 tablespoons sugar
1/2 cup butter
Whipped cream (made from
    1 cup cream)
Raspberry or currant jelly
    (garnish)

1. Cook apples in water to make applesauce. Add 3/4 cup sugar; set aside.

2. Mix bread crumbs with 2 tablespoons sugar. Melt butter in a heavy skillet. Add crumbs and cook, stirring until browned and crisp; cool.

3. Spread a layer of crumbs in the bottom of a serving dish. Cover with a layer of applesauce. Repeat layers until all is used, ending with a layer of bread crumbs. Chill.

4. Cover the top of the cake with whipped cream, and dab with jelly. Use any remaining whipped cream to top individual servings.

Yield: About 12 servings.

---

*The Pennsylvania Dutch are expert at making
dried apple slices, which they call "schnitz."*

Apple Bonnie

6 large apples (preferably
   McIntosh), sliced
1 tablespoon fresh lemon
   juice
1 cup butter
1 (2-layer size) package
   yellow cake mix
1/2 cup flaked coconut
1 dozen marshmallows

1. Arrange apples in a 13x9x2-inch pan. Sprinkle with lemon juice.

2. Blend butter into dry cake mix until crumbly; mix in coconut and sprinkle over top of apples.

3. Arrange marshmallows, about 2 inches apart, over the cake mix topping.

4. Bake at 350 degrees for about 40 minutes. Cool slightly and cut into squares.

Yield: 28 squares.

*Over 8000 apple varieties are known throughout history.
More than 2500 of them can be found in America.*

Apple Cheese Cake

4 ounces cream cheese,
   softened
1/2 cup butter
1 egg
3/4 cup sugar
1 cup flour
1 teaspoon baking powder
3 apples, sliced
1/2 cup brown sugar
1 teaspoon cinnamon

1. Beat cream cheese and butter together until creamy. Add egg and sugar and beat until very fluffy.

2. Sift together flour and baking powder, and gently fold into cheese mixture.

3. Spoon into a deep 9-inch pie plate which has been well buttered and dusted with flour.

4. Cover the top with apple slices, pinwheel fashion.

5. Sprinkle with mixture of brown sugar and cinnamon. Bake at 350 degrees for 40 to 45 minutes. Serve warm with sweetened whipped cream.

Yield: One 9-inch cake.

Note: *Maple sugar makes an elegant substitute for the brown sugar.*

---

*You can keep brown sugar moist and soft
by including an apple in the container.*

Apple Pound Cake

Batter:
3 cups flour
1 teaspoon baking soda
1 teaspoon salt
1 teaspoon cinnamon
1-1/2 cups vegetable oil
2 cups sugar
3 eggs
2 teaspoons vanilla
2 cups grated apples
1 cup finely chopped pecans

Topping:
1/2 cup butter
1/2 cup light brown sugar
2 teaspoons milk

1. For Batter: Thoroughly stir together the flour, baking soda, salt, and cinnamon. In a large bowl beat together until combined the oil, sugar, eggs, and vanilla. Gradually beat in dry ingredients until smooth. Fold in apples and pecans.

2. Turn into a buttered and floured 10x4-inch Bundt pan. Bake at 325 degrees for 1 hour and 20 minutes. Place cake, still in the pan, on a wire rack to cool for 20 minutes.

3. For Topping: About 5 minutes before the cake has finished cooling, bring the butter, brown sugar, and milk to a boil in a small saucepan, stirring constantly; boil for 2 minutes.

4. With a small spatula, loosen cake around the edges and around the tube. Turn out on a wire rack. At once spoon the hot sugar mixture over the still warm cake, allowing it to run down the sides. Cool completely. (For a day or two, this cake may be stored at room temperature in a tightly covered tin; for longer storage, cover and refrigerate, but bring to room temperature before serving.)

Yield: One 10-inch Bundt cake.

Dutch Apple Cake

Batter:
2-1/2 cups flour
2 teaspoons baking powder
2 tablespoons sugar
1 cup butter
1 teaspoon vanilla
1 egg, slightly beaten
6 cooking apples, sliced

Topping:
1-1/2 cups sugar
2-1/2 tablespoons flour
1/2 teaspoon salt
1/4 cup butter
1 teaspoon cinnamon

Orange Sauce:
1 cup sugar
2 tablespoons cornstarch
1 teaspoon salt
1 cup water
2 tablespoons butter
1 (6-ounce) can frozen
    orange juice concentrate,
    undiluted

1. **For Batter:** Sift dry ingredients together; cut in butter until mixture is crumbly. Add vanilla to egg; blend with flour mixture. Press evenly onto the bottom and sides of a 15x10x1-inch pan. Cover dough with overlapping layers of apple slices.

2. **For Topping:** Combine ingredients and sprinkle over apples.

3. Bake at 350 degrees for 45 minutes, or until apples are tender and topping is golden brown. Cut into squares. Serve warm or cold with whipped cream or with Orange Sauce.

4. **For Orange Sauce:** Combine sugar, cornstarch, and salt in a saucepan. Add water slowly, stirring constantly. Add butter and bring to a boil. Reduce heat and continue cooking until mixture thickens. Remove from heat and stir in orange juice concentrate. Serve warm or chilled.

Yield: 12 to 16 servings.

Note: To make Lemon Sauce, make with frozen lemonade concentrate; omit sugar. To make Apple Sauce, substitute 1 cup apple juice for water; eliminate frozen orange juice concentrate.

Goddess Tribute

Batter:
6 tablespoons butter
3 tablespoons sugar
2 egg yolks
3/4 cup plus 2 tablespoons
  flour
6 tablespoons finely chopped
  blanched almonds
3 tablespoons grated lemon
  rind

Topping:
5 tablespoons sugar
2 tablespoons lemon juice
5 apples, halved
6 tablespoons raspberry jam

Meringue:
4 egg whites
Dash of salt
1/2 cup sugar

1. For Batter: Cream butter and sugar together. Add egg yolks and beat vigorously. Stir in flour, almonds, and lemon rind; blend well. Press dough onto the bottom of an 8-inch square pan. Brush with slightly beaten egg white (use a small amount of the egg white from which the meringue is to be made). Bake at 350 degrees for 15 minutes or until crust is golden brown. Cool in pan.

2. For Topping: Combine sugar and lemon juice in a skillet. Add apple halves; cover tightly and cook over low heat until apples are just tender. Spread the cooled crust with jam, then arrange apples on top.

3. For Meringue: Beat egg whites and salt until frothy; add sugar gradually, beating constantly; continue beating until peaks are formed. Pile meringue lightly over apples. Bake at 350 degrees for 15 minutes.

Yield: 9 to 12 servings.

*Greek and Roman myths refer to the apple
as a symbol of love and beauty.*

Quick Apple Kuchen

1/2 cup butter
1 (2-layer size) package
    yellow cake mix
1/2 cup flaked coconut
6 large apples, thinly sliced
1/2 cup sugar
1 teaspoon cinnamon
2 egg yolks or 1 whole egg
1 cup sour cream

1. Cut butter into dry cake mix until crumbly. Stir in coconut. Pat into a 13x9x2-inch pan; build up edge slightly. Bake at 350 degrees for 10 minutes.

2. Arrange apples on the baked crust while it is still warm. Mix sugar and cinnamon; sprinkle over apples.

3. Beat egg yolks and mix with sour cream; spread over apples. Bake at 350 degrees for 25 minutes or until apples are cooked through. Do not overbake.

Yield: About 15 servings.

 *FAST APPLE FAVORITE*

Extra-Moist Chocolate Cake

In your favorite devil's food cake mix, substitute applesauce in place of oil or water. Tastes good and keeps moist.

Sherry Apple Cake Superb

Batter:
1 cup butter
2 cups sugar
3 eggs
3 cups flour
1-1/2 teaspoons baking
    soda
1/2 teaspoon salt
1 teaspoon cinnamon
1/8 teaspoon nutmeg
3 cups chopped apples
2 cups chopped walnuts
    or pecans
2 teaspoons vanilla

Glaze:
1-1/2 cups sugar
1/4 cup butter
1/2 cup sherry

1. For Batter: Cream butter and sugar together well. Add eggs, one at a time, beating well after each addition.

2. Combine dry ingredients; sift and add gradually, mixing until well blended. Add apples, nuts, and vanilla.

3. Pour into a buttered and floured Bundt pan or 10-inch tube pan. Bake at 325 degrees for 1-1/2 hours or until a cake tester inserted in the center of the cake comes out clean. Let stand for 15 minutes; remove from pan.

4. For Glaze: Combine sugar, butter, and sherry in a small saucepan. Mix and stir over low heat until butter melts and sugar dissolves.

5. Prick the cake well all over with a fork. Slowly pour the glaze over the cake until absorbed.

Yield: One 10-inch cake.

Bavarian Apple Almond Torte

Torte:
1/2 cup butter
3 eggs
1 cup sugar
1-1/2 cups blanched
   almonds, finely ground
2 tablespoons flour

Topping:
3 red-skinned apples,
   unpeeled
3 tablespoons butter
1 tablespoon brown sugar
2 tablespoons red jelly
   (currant or other)

Custard:
1/4 cup sugar
1 tablespoon cornstarch
1/4 teaspoon salt
1 cup milk
1 egg yolk, beaten
1 tablespoon butter
1/2 teaspoon almond
   extract

1. For Torte: Butter a 9-inch cake pan, line it with wax paper, and butter the paper. Cream butter until very light and fluffy. Beat eggs and sugar until foamy. Alternately add creamed butter and ground almonds to eggs and sugar, mixing well after each addition. Stir in flour and pour into pan. Bake at 350 degrees for 30 to 35 minutes. Turn out onto a wire rack and cool. Invert onto a serving dish and remove wax paper.

2. For Custard: Combine sugar, cornstarch, and salt in a sauce-pan. Slowly stir in milk. Bring to a boil, stirring constantly; boil for 1 minute. Stir half of the mixture into the egg yolk. Blend into remaining mixture and cook for 1 more minute. Remove from heat; stir in butter and almond extract. Cool and spread over torte. Refrigerate torte.

3. For Topping: Core and cut each apple into three 1/2-inch slices, discarding end pieces. Brown butter with brown sugar in a large skillet. Sauté apple slices on both sides until just soft. Cool slightly; arrange overlapping slices on top of custard. Melt jelly and spoon over apples.

Yield: 8 to 10 servings.

Apple Apricot Torte

Dough:
1-1/2 cups flour
1 teaspoon baking powder
2 tablespoons sugar
1 egg, slightly beaten
1/2 cup butter, softened

Filling:
3 cups finely chopped
   apples
1 cup dried apricots, cut
   into thin strips
1 teaspoon cinnamon
1-1/2 cups sugar
3 eggs, slightly beaten
1 cup sour cream
1/4 cup finely chopped
   almonds

1. For Dough: Sift together flour, baking powder, and sugar. Add egg and butter; work into flour mixture until a smooth dough is formed. Press dough into a thin layer on the bottom and sides of a buttered 9-inch springform pan, making the sides 2 inches high.

2. For Filling: Combine apples, apricots, cinnamon, and sugar. Combine eggs and sour cream; blend until smooth. Add to apple mixture and mix well.

3. Pour filling into the dough-lined pan and sprinkle with the almonds. Bake at 350 degrees for 1-1/4 hours. Cool and remove from pan.

Yield: 12 servings.

Apples are best stored in the refrigerator to prevent decay and to maintain quality, juiciness, and crispness.

Viennese Apple Strudel

Dough:
1 cup butter
3 cups flour
1/2 cup confectioners'sugar
2 eggs, separated
6 tablespoons milk

Garnish:
Whipped cream
Maraschino cherries

Filling:
1/2 cup buttered bread
  crumbs
4 cups thinly sliced apples
1/4 cup honey
4 sugar cubes, coarsely
  crushed
1/4 cup plumped golden
  raisins
1/4 cup finely slivered
  almonds
1 teaspoon grated orange
  rind
1 tablespoon orange juice

1. **For Dough:** Cut butter finely into combined flour and sugar. Combine egg yolks and milk; stir gradually into mixture; form dough into a ball. Roll out into a 17x13-inch rectangle.

2. **For Filling:** Sprinkle buttered crumbs over the dough; arrange slightly overlapping apple slices over the center of the rectangle. Combine honey, crushed sugar cubes, raisins, almonds, orange rind, and orange juice; spoon over apples, pressing down gently. Draw one side of the dough over the filling; top with the remaining side. Seal edges.

3. Arrange the strudel on a baking sheet; brush the top with slightly beaten egg whites. Bake at 350 degrees for 45 minutes or until flaky and golden.

4. **For Garnish:** Using a pastry tube, press ruffles of whipped cream in four rows. Garnish whipped cream with whole and chopped maraschino cherries as desired.

Yield: 16 servings.

Notes: For buttered bread crumbs, combine 1/2 cup dry plain bread crumbs with 1 tablespoon melted butter. To plump raisins, cover with boiling water; let stand for 10 minutes; drain well.

Mini Apple Strudels

2 apples, finely chopped
1/2 teaspoon cinnamon
2 teaspoons sugar
1/2 cup walnuts, chopped
1/4 cup dark brown sugar
1/2 cup flour
1/4 teaspoon cinnamon
1/4 cup butter, softened
1 (3-ounce) package cream
    cheese, softened
1 (8-ounce) package Crescent
    Dinner Rolls

1. In a small bowl, combine apples, 1/2 teaspoon cinnamon, sugar, and walnuts; blend well. Set aside.

2. In another bowl, combine brown sugar, flour, 1/4 teaspoon cinnamon, and butter; mix until crumbly. Set aside.

3. Separate Crescent Dinner Rolls into eight triangles. Spread each triangle with softened cream cheese; spoon a heaping tablespoon of the apple mixture over that; then roll very carefully into a crescent shape as directed on the package, tucking ends under.

4. Sprinkle with the brown sugar mixture. Place on a greased baking sheet with tucked ends on the underside. Repeat until all eight are made.

5. Bake at 375 degrees for 10 to 12 mintues. Serve hot or cold.

Yield: 8 miniature strudels.

Apple Napoleons

1 (10-ounce) package (6)
   frozen patty shells,
   thawed
2 cups grated apples
1-1/2 cups sifted
   confectioners' sugar
1/4 teaspoon nutmeg
1 cup whipped cream or
   refrigerated whipped
   topping
1/2 cup chopped walnuts
3 to 4 teaspoons milk
1/2 teaspoon almond
   extract

1. Place three patty shells on a floured board and place the remaining three shells on top of them. Roll out to form a 12x8-inch rectangle. Cut into eight 3x4-inch rectangles. Bake on an ungreased baking sheet at 400 degrees for 15 to 20 minutes or until golden brown. Cool.

2. While the pastry is baking, combine apples, 1/2 cup of the sugar, nutmeg, whipped cream, and nuts. Split open the cooled pastry rectangles horizontally. Place some of the apple mixture on the bottom half of each pastry rectangle; cover with the top half.

3. Combine remaining 1 cup sugar with milk and almond extract. Spoon this glaze over the top of each napoleon.

Yield: 8 napoleons.

Eat an apple
On going to bed
And you'll keep the doctor
From earning his bread.
Unknown

Apple Pastry Logs

Pastry:
1/2 cup butter
1 cup flour
1 egg yolk, beaten
1/4 cup sour cream

Filling:
1 cup orange marmalade
4 apples, cut into 1/4-inch
  slices
2 tablespoons sugar
1/3 cup shredded coconut
1/3 cup chopped walnuts
Confectioners' sugar

1. **For Pastry:** Cut butter into flour until mixture resembles small crumbs. Combine egg yolk and sour cream; mix with flour until dough forms a ball. Divide dough in half; chill at least 3 hours or overnight.

2. Roll out each ball of dough into a 12x9-inch rectangle.

3. Use half of the filling ingredients for each log. Spread marmalade along the long edge of each dough rectangle. Arrange two or three layers of apples in a single row on the marmalade. Sprinkle with sugar, then with coconut and nuts.

4. Lift pastry near the filling side and roll. Place on a lightly greased baking sheet, seam side down. Moisten with milk to seal, tucking ends under.

5. Bake at 350 degrees for about 25 minutes or until browned. Juices will probably run, so remove gently from pan. Sprinkle with confectioners' sugar. Serve warm. May be reheated.

Yield: Two 12-inch logs.

Dried apple peels thrown into a fireplace blaze
will fill the air with a sweet aroma.

Notes

APPLE DESSERTS

Baked Apples
Cookies
Crêpes
Puddings
Confections

Ricotta-Stuffed Apples

8 baking apples, unpeeled
1/2 cup minced blanched
    almonds
2 ounces unsweetened or
    sweet chocolate, grated
8 amaretti or small
    macaroons, crushed
1 egg yolk
10 tablespoons ricotta
    cheese
6 tablespoons sugar
6 tablespoons Marsala

1. Core each apple three quarters of the way down; with a spoon, scoop out some of the pulp.

2. Combine minced almonds, grated chocolate, crushed amaretti, egg yolk, ricotta, and sugar. Add 2 tablespoons of Marsala and stuff the apples with the mixture.

3. Make small slits in the apple skins.

4. Pour the remaining 4 tablespoons Marsala into a baking dish. Set the apples into the dish and bake at 350 degrees for about 30 minutes, or until the skins are soft.

Yield: 8 servings.

Use a round metal measuring spoon (teaspoon size)
as an apple corer and baller. Cut the apple in half
and use the spoon to scoop out the core.

Apple Blossom

4 baking apples
2/3 cup raisins
2/3 cup chopped pecans
3 tablespoons sherry or
  orange juice
1/2 cup brown sugar
Butter
Whipped cream (garnish)
Red sugar sprinkles (optional)

1. Butter 4 medium-sized custard dishes. Core, then peel apples part of the way down, creating a petal effect. Mix together raisins, chopped pecans, and sherry. Spoon this mixture inside the area created by the petals.

2. Sprinkle top with brown sugar and dot generously with butter.

3. Bake at 350 degrees for about 25 minutes, or until apples are just done, not too hard or too soft.

4. When ready to serve, top with whipped cream and red sugar sprinkles, if desired.

Yield: 4 servings.

Apples do not reproduce true from seed.
Each tree must be bud-grafted.

Apple Dumplings

2 cups flour
2 teaspoons baking powder
1 teaspoon salt
1 tablespoon sugar
2 tablespoons butter
2/3 cup milk
6 baking apples
1/2 cup sugar
1 teaspoon nutmeg

1. Sift dry ingredients together; cut in butter until mixture is slightly coarser than cornmeal. Mix in milk quickly with a fork, adding more if necessary so the dough holds together.

2. Pat and roll out lightly on a floured board into a rectangle about 10x15 inches and about 1/4 inch thick. Cut into six 5x5-inch squares.

3. Place one apple on each square of dough; sprinkle with combined sugar and nutmeg. Draw the four corners of the dough together on top of each apple and pinch the edges together. Prick with a fork and bake at 350 degrees for 30 to 45 minutes or until lightly browned.

Yield: 6 servings.

Notes: For variety, fill the center of the apples with homemade or canned whole cranberry sauce. When serving, top with hot cranberry sauce, thinned slightly with water, and seasoned with nutmeg and cloves if desired.

---

*Coleridge holds that a man cannot have a pure mind
who refuses apple dumplings.*
Charles Lamb, Grace before Meat

Apple Raisin Cookies

Dough:
1/2 cup butter
1-1/3 cups brown sugar
1 egg
2 cups flour
1/2 teaspoon salt
1 teaspoon baking soda
1/2 cup milk
1 cup unpeeled, finely
   chopped apples
1 cup raisins
1 cup chopped nuts
   (optional)

Glaze:
1-1/2 cups confectioners'
   sugar
4 teaspoons milk
1 teaspoon melted butter
1/4 teaspoon vanilla
Dash of salt

1. For Dough: Cream together butter, sugar, and egg. Combine dry ingredients; add half to the creamed mixture, and then blend in milk. Add remaining dry ingredients. Mix well.

2. Mix in apples, raisins, and nuts. Drop by teaspoonfuls onto a buttered cookie sheet. Bake at 350 degrees for 10 to 12 minutes.

3. For Glaze: Combine confectioners' sugar, milk, melted butter, vanilla, and salt. Mix until creamy; spread on cookies.

Yield: About 4 dozen cookies.

---

*The secret to moist cookies is to keep
an apple in the cookie jar.*

Apple Date Squares

Dough:
1/2 cup butter
3/4 cup sugar
1 egg
1-1/2 cups flour
1 teaspoon baking soda
1/4 teaspoon salt
2 cups finely chopped
    apples
1 cup chopped dates

Topping:
1/4 cup brown sugar
1 teaspoon cinnamon
1/2 cup chopped nuts

1. For Dough: Cream together butter and sugar; add egg and beat well. Sift together flour, baking soda, and salt, and blend into creamed mixture.

2. Stir in apples and dates; spread into a greased 9-inch square baking dish.

3. For Topping: Combine ingredients and sprinkle evenly over the apple mixture.

4. Bake at 350 degrees for 30 to 35 minutes. Cut into squares. May be served warm with vanilla ice cream.

Yield: 16 squares.

*The first commercial apple nursery was established
in Flushing, New York (on Long Island) in 1730.*

Apple Butterscotch Squares

2 to 3 large apples, grated
1/2 cup butter
3/4 cup brown sugar
2 eggs
1/2 cup sour cream
1/2 cup milk
1 teaspoon vanilla
2 cups flour
1 teaspoon baking soda
Dash of salt
1 cup butterscotch chips

1. Cream together butter and sugar; blend in eggs, sour cream, milk, and vanilla. Sift dry ingredients together and blend into creamed mixture.

2. Add grated apples and butterscotch chips. Spread batter into a buttered 9-inch square baking pan. Bake at 350 degrees for about 45 minutes or until lightly browned. Cut into squares.

Yield: 25 squares.

Apple orchards exist wherever the summer climate
is moderate and the wintertime provides
a dormant period for the trees.

Apple Hermits

1 cup sugar
1/2 cup vegetable oil
3 cups flour
1-1/2 teaspoons cinnamon
1/2 teaspoon nutmeg
1/2 teaspoon salt
1 teaspoon baking soda
1/4 cup molasses
1/4 cup black coffee
1/2 cup milk
1 cup diced apples
3/4 cup raisins
Sugar

1. Cream together sugar and vegetable oil. Sift dry ingredients together.

2. Combine molasses, coffee, and milk, and add to creamed mixture alternately with the dry ingredients.

3. Fold in apples and raisins. The batter will be stiff; spread it in strips across two greased cookie sheets. Bake at 350 degrees for 20 to 25 minutes.

3. Dust with sugar while still warm; cut into squares.

Yield: About 40 hermits.

An apple tree's productive life is from about 6 years to its peak at about 35 to 40 years.

Buttery Caramel Apple Squares

1 (11-ounce) package pie
    crust mix
1/2 cup granulated brown
    sugar
1 cup quick oats
3/4 cup chopped walnuts
3 tablespoons butter, melted
1/4 cup cold water
2 tablespoons cornstarch
3 tablespoons sugar
4 apples, grated
1 (12-ounce) jar caramel
    topping

1. Very lightly butter a 13x9x2-inch baking pan on the bottom and 1 inch up the sides.

2. Combine pie crust mix, brown sugar, oats, and nuts; drizzle with 2 tablespoons of the melted butter and the water. Stir with a fork until evenly combined. Reserve 1-1/2 cups of this mixture.

3. Press the remaining crumb mixture into the prepared pan, covering the bottom of the pan and 1/4 inch up the sides.

4. Sprinkle cornstarch and sugar over apples; stir to combine. Spoon apples evenly over crust. Combine remaining 1 table-spoon melted butter with caramel topping; drizzle over apples. Crumble reserved crumb mixture evenly over apples.

5. Bake at 375 degrees for 35 to 40 minutes or until topping is golden brown. When cool, cut into 2-inch squares.

Yield: 24 squares.

Divine Apple Squares

2-1/2 cups flour
1 tablespoon sugar
1 teaspoon salt
1 cup butter
1 egg, separated
Milk
2/3 cup crushed cornflakes
4 cups sliced apples
1 cup sugar
1-1/2 teaspoons cinnamon,
    or to taste

Glaze:
1 cup confectioners' sugar
2 tablespoons lemon juice

1. Sift flour, 1 tablespoon sugar, and salt together; cut in butter. Place egg yolk in a measuring cup; add milk to make 1/3 cup liquid. Add to flour mixture; mix just enough for dough to shape into a ball.

2. Roll out half the dough into a 15x11-inch rectangle; transfer to a rimmed baking sheet. Cover with crushed cornflakes; spread with apples. Mix 1 cup sugar with cinnamon; sprinkle over apples.

3. Roll remaining dough for the top crust; place over apples, pinching edges together. Cut steam vents in the crust. Beat egg white until stiff; spread over the top crust. Bake at 400 degrees for 40 minutes.

4. **For Glaze:** Combine confectioners' sugar and lemon juice. Drizzle over the hot crust.

5. Cut into squares.

Yield: 16 squares.

Note: This recipe freezes beautifully and can also be cut into smaller squares for afternoon tea.

Apple-Stuffed Crêpes

Crêpes:
2 eggs
2 tablespoons vegetable oil
1 cup milk
3/4 cup sifted flour
1/2 teaspoon salt
2 tablespoons sugar
1/2 teaspoon brandy extract
Butter to cook crêpes
Confectioners' sugar
(garnish)

Filling:
2 pounds tart cooking
apples, sliced
1/2 cup water
3/4 cup finely chopped
walnuts
1 teaspoon lemon juice
1/4 teaspoon cinnamon
1/4 teaspoon nutmeg
1/2 cup maple syrup
Sugar to taste

1. For Crêpes: In medium bowl, beat together eggs, vegetable oil, and milk. Add remaining ingredients and beat until very smooth. Refrigerate, covered, for at least 1 hour.

2. For Filling: Place apples in a saucepan with water, walnuts, lemon juice, cinnamon, and nutmeg. Bring to boil; reduce heat and simmer, covered, for about 20 minutes. Add maple syrup, and sugar if desired. Cook until the mixture is very thick. Keep warm.

3. In a 7-inch skillet, melt 1 teaspoon butter over medium heat. When butter is hot, add 1-1/2 tablespoons batter, rotating the pan quickly to cover the bottom. Cook for 1 minute on each side or until golden brown. Repeat with remaining batter. Keep crêpes warm in the oven at 200 degrees.

4. Lightly spread about 3 tablespoons of the apple filling on each crêpe. Roll up crêpes and place on a warm serving dish. Sprinkle with confectioners' sugar. Serve warm.

Yield: 20 crêpes.

Ricotta Apple Roll-Ups

Crêpes:
1-1/2 cups flour
1 tablespoon sugar
2 teaspoons baking powder
1/2 teaspoon salt
1 egg, beaten until thick
1-1/2 cups milk
2 tablespoons butter, melted
  and cooled
1 large apple, grated
1/2 teaspoon vanilla
Butter to cook crêpes

Filling:
2 cups ricotta cheese
1 cup sour cream
2 teaspoons sugar

Apple-Apple Sauce:
4 apples, quartered
1/4 cup sugar
1/4 cup pineapple juice
Nutmeg

1. For Crêpes: Sift together dry ingredients. Combine beaten egg, milk, melted butter, and grated apple. Add liquid ingredients to dry ingredients and beat with a rotary beater until smooth. Add vanilla.

2. Lightly butter a 6-inch skillet and spoon 1/4 cup batter into skillet. Spread batter quickly with a spoon. Cook over medium heat until lightly browned. Flip crêpe and brown on other side. Repeat with rest of batter. Keep crêpes warm in the oven at 200 degrees.

3. For Filling: Combine ricotta cheese, sour cream, and sugar. Drop about 3 tablespoons of filling into the center of each crêpe. Roll up crêpes and place on a warm serving dish.

4. For Apple-Apple Sauce: Place apples, sugar, and pineapple juice in a blender. Process until a thick sauce is formed. Pour into a saucepan and bring to a boil. Pour sauce over crêpes or serve separately. Dust with nutmeg.

Yield: 12 crêpes.

Diet-Breaker Dessert

1 egg, beaten
2 tablespoons flour
1/2 cup maple syrup
1 cup sour cream
1/2 teaspoon maple flavor
4 cups apples, sliced

Topping:
1 cup butter
1 cup brown sugar
1 egg
1-1/2 cups flour
1 teaspoon baking soda
1/2 teaspoon salt
1 cup sour cream
1/2 teaspoon maple flavor

1. Mix beaten egg well with 2 tablespoons flour, maple syrup, sour cream, maple flavor, and apples. Spoon into a greased 10-inch pan.

2. For Topping: Cream together butter and sugar; add egg and beat until light and fluffy. Sift dry ingredients together and add to creamed mixture along with sour cream and maple flavor; beat until smooth.

3. Pour topping over apple mixture. Bake at 350 degrees for about 45 minutes. Serve with cream or ice cream.

Yield: 9 to 12 servings.

Stay me with flagons,
Comfort me with apples;
For I am sick with love.
The Song of Solomon

Apple Cobbler

4 cups sliced baking apples
1 cup sugar
1/8 teaspoon cinnamon
1/2 teaspoon almond extract
    (optional)
2 tablespoons butter
1-1/2 cups sifted flour
2 teaspoons baking powder
1/3 cup sugar
1/2 teaspoon salt
1/4 cup butter
1 egg, beaten
2/3 cup milk

1. Place apples into a 1-1/2-quart baking dish. Sprinkle with 1 cup sugar, cinnamon, and almond extract; dot with 2 tablespoons butter.

2. Sift flour, baking powder, 1/3 cup sugar, and salt into mixing bowl. Cut in 1/4 cup butter until mixture is slightly coarser than cornmeal.

3. Combine egg and milk; add to dry ingredients and blend just enough to combine. Spoon mixture over the apples in the baking dish.

4. Bake at 425 degrees for about 30 minutes or until browned. Serve with fresh cream, sour cream, or ice cream if desired.

Yield: 6 to 8 servings.

---

*Apples help to clean the teeth and provide roughage;
they are high in potassium and low in sodium,
and are a source of natural sugar.*

Apple Crisp

4 cups sliced apples
1/3 cup water
2/3 cup flour
1 cup brown sugar
1/2 teaspoon cinnamon
1/4 teaspoon nutmeg
Dash of salt
1/3 cup butter

1. Butter a 1-1/2-quart or deep pie dish. Add apples and pour in water.

2. Mix remaining ingredients, cutting in butter with a fork or pastry blender. Sprinkle mixture evenly over apples.

3. Bake at 350 degrees for about 30 minutes or until topping is browned and apples are tender when pierced with fork.

4. Serve warm with ice cream, whipped cream, or plain cream.

Yield: 8 to 10 servings.

Note: For a tangy apple-cranberry crisp, substitute about 1-1/2 cups chopped fresh cranberries for 2 cups of the sliced apples. You may want to add a bit more sugar.

Apple Charlotte

8 tablespoons butter
8 apples, sliced
6 tablespoons sugar
1 tablespoon lemon juice
1 teaspoon grated lemon rind
6 or more slices white bread
1/2 cup raisins

1. Melt 2 tablespoons of the butter in a heavy skillet and cook apples for about 20 minutes until soft but not mushy. Stir in sugar, lemon juice, and lemon rind.

2. Cut crusts off bread and cut each slice lengthwise into 3 pieces. Melt remaining 6 tablespoons butter; dip each piece of bread into butter and use to line a 1-quart shallow glass baking dish. (The bread slices should be arranged on the bottom and then up the sides of the dish so that the edges of the bread are touching.)

3. Combine apples with raisins and spoon into the bread-lined dish. Bake at 350 degrees for about 40 minutes or until bread is golden brown.

4. Let cool slightly, then unmold. Cut in slices and serve warm. Good with ice cream.

Yield: 8 or more servings.

*To make apples ripen faster, keep them in a crisper
for a few days and then keep them outside
the crisper until they are ripe.*

Apple Bread Pudding

1-3/4 cups milk
1/2 teaspoon vanilla
2 eggs, slightly beaten
2 cups bread cubes or
    chunks
2/3 cup raisins
1 cup brown sugar
3 apples, sliced

1. Combine milk, vanilla, and eggs. Pour over bread in a bowl, and let soften if bread is stale. Add raisins.

2. Sprinkle brown sugar into a buttered 1-1/2-quart baking dish; arrange sliced apples over, pressing slightly into sugar.

3. Pour bread mixture over apples and sugar. Bake at 325 degrees for about 60 minutes or until set.

4. If desired, the pudding may be inverted so that the apples are on top. To achieve this effect, slide a spatula around the edge of the dish to loosen, and turn the pudding out onto a plate.

Yield: 8 servings.

Note: *This recipe may be prepared in the top of a double boiler: cook over simmering water for about 1 hour.*

---

*Water does not cling to apples on trees because they have
a natural coat that helps reduce moisture loss and
protect the fruit from insects and disease.*

Apple Supreme

1/4 cup butter
1/2 cup sugar
1/4 teaspoon salt
3 eggs, separated
2 tablespoons lemon juice
4 tart apples, grated

1. Cream butter and sugar together. Add salt and egg yolks and beat until well blended. Add the lemon juice, a little at a time, and then the grated apples.

2. Beat egg whites until stiff; fold into apple mixture and pour into a buttered casserole. Bake at 350 degrees for 35 to 40 minutes.

3. This is best served with whipped cream, but may also be served with fresh or frozen strawberries or with plain cream.

Yield: 5 or 6 servings.

It was from out the rind of one apple tasted
That the knowledge of good and evil
As two twins cleaving together
Leaped forth into the world.
Milton, Areopagitica

Fresh Apple Mousse

1/2 cup sugar
1/2 cup water
1/2 teaspoon vanilla
2 cups sliced apples
1 cup heavy cream
1 tablespoon sugar
1 teaspoon vanilla
1-1/2 cups crushed peanut
    brittle

1. Combine 1/2 cup sugar, water, and 1/2 teaspoon vanilla in a saucepan. Bring to a slow boil. Add apple slices and simmer slowly until tender and transparent, about 2 to 5 minutes. Remove apple slices from syrup; let cool.

2. Whip cream, adding 1 tablespoon sugar and 1 teaspoon vanilla. Fold apple slices carefully into whipped cream.

3. Spoon a layer of the apple cream mixture into parfait glasses and sprinkle with a little crushed peanut brittle. Repeat layers, ending with peanut brittle. Chill for 4 to 5 hours or overnight.

Yield: 4 to 6 servings.

Send kisses with apples, and I will feast with pleasure.
Petronius

Apple Indian Pudding

1/2 cup yellow cornmeal
1 quart milk, scalded
2/3 cup molasses
1 teaspoon cinnamon or
    ginger
1 teaspoon salt
2 tart apples, sliced
2 cups cold milk

1. Add cornmeal slowly to hot milk in the top of a double boiler. Cook over boiling water, stirring constantly, until thick. Stir in molasses, cinnamon, and salt.

2. Place alternate layers of mixture and apples into a buttered baking dish. Pour cold milk on top. Bake at 300 degrees for 2 hours or longer. Serve with hard sauce or vanilla ice cream, if desired.

Yield: 8 to 10 servings.

*The first apples grown in the United States were
probably obtained from trees planted in
Boston, Massachusetts, from which
the "fair pippins" were plucked
on October 16, 1639.*

Apple Kugel

Kugel:
8 ounces fine noodles,
   cooked
1/2 cup melted butter
2 apples, sliced
3 eggs, lightly beaten
1/2 cup dark corn syrup
1/2 cup golden raisins
1/3 cup sugar
1/2 teaspoon cinnamon
1 teaspoon vanilla
1/3 cup orange juice
1 tablespoon lemon juice
1/2 cup crushed cornflakes

Topping:
2/3 cup crushed cornflakes
2/3 cup sugar
1 teaspoon cinnamon
1/2 cup crushed walnuts

1. For Kugel: Combine all ingredients except crushed cornflakes.

2. Butter a 7-1/2x13-inch pan. Sprinkle with 1/2 cup crushed cornflakes. Pour noodle mixture into pan.

3. For Topping: Combine ingredients and sprinkle over kugel.

4. Bake at 350 degrees for 30 minutes. Serve hot or cold.

Yield: 12 to 16 servings.

Note: Graham cracker crumbs may substituted for crushed cornflakes.

Apple Noodle Pudding

3 eggs, beaten
4 tablespoons melted butter
1/4 cup sugar
1/2 teaspoon salt
1/2 cup sour cream
1 cup milk
1/2 teaspoon vanilla
4 ounces farmers' cheese,
    softened

1/2 pound cottage cheese
1 3-ounce package cream
    cheese, softened
8 ounces wide egg noodles
1-1/2 cups chopped apples
Cinnamon
Brown sugar
Butter

1. Beat eggs with butter, sugar, salt, sour cream, milk, and vanilla. Mix cheeses together; add to egg mixture. Mix well and add noodles. Stir in chopped apples. Pour into a buttered 13x9x2-inch pan.

2. Bake at 350 degrees for 45 minutes. Sprinkle with cinnamon and brown sugar to taste and dot with butter. Bake for 30 minutes longer. Cool and cut into squares. Serve warm. May also be served with a spoonful of sour cream on top.

Yield: 18 servings.

My heart is like an apple tree
Whose boughs are bent with thick-set fruit.
Dante Gabriel Rossetti, A Birthday

Fruit Noodle Pudding

1 pound egg noodles,
 cooked
1/2 cup butter
8 apples, sliced
1 (16-ounce) can whole
 cranberry sauce
3 tablespoons sugar
Cinnamon to taste
1/2 cup crushed cornflakes
Sugar and cinnamon to taste
4 eggs
2 cups pineapple juice

1. Drain noodles and add butter. Place one third of the noodles into a buttered 13x9x2-inch pan. Add half the apples and half the cranberry sauce and sprinkle with combined sugar and cinnamon.

2. Layer another third of the noodles, and then the remaining apples, cranberry sauce, and sugar and cinnamon. Add a third layer of noodles; cover with crushed cornflakes mixed with sugar and cinnamon.

3. Beat eggs; add pineapple juice. Spoon over noodles. Bake at 350 degrees for 1-1/4 hours.

Yield: 10 to 16 servings.

---

*In early twentieth-century New Orleans, apples were
used as magic objects in voodoo ceremonies
when love was the goal.*

Apple Baked Alaska

5 apples, thinly sliced
3 tablespoons sugar
2 teaspoons cornstarch
1/2 teaspoon each nutmeg
   and cinnamon
1/4 teaspoon salt
1 quart vanilla ice cream,
   softened slightly

Meringue:
3 egg whites
1/8 teaspoon cream of tartar
1/4 cup confectioners' sugar

1. Arrange sliced apples in a 9-inch pie plate. Combine sugar, cornstarch, spices, and salt; sprinkle evenly over apples. Cover with aluminum foil; bake at 425 degrees for 30 minutes or until apples are just tender. Remove from oven, cool, and refrigerate.

2. At serving time, cover with an even layer of ice cream; place in the freezer.

3. **For Meringue:** While ice cream is hardening in the freezer, beat egg whites with cream of tartar until frothy. Gradually add confectioners' sugar, a tablespoon at a time, and continue beating until the mixture stands in peaks.

4. Spread meringue over the ice cream, making sure to spread it to the rim of the pie plate so that the edges are sealed. Place the pie plate in a roasting pan, and surround the pie plate with ice cubes. Bake at 500 degrees for 3 minutes or until lightly browned.

Yield: 8 to 10 servings.

Note: If time permits, keep the apples covered with ice cream in the freezer until the ice cream is really hardened and the apples are well chilled.

Apple Frozen Yogurt

1 cup plain yogurt
1/2 cup sugar
Dash of salt
4 egg whites, slightly beaten
1/2 teaspoon vanilla
1 cup applesauce
1 cup whipping cream

1. Heat yogurt in a heavy saucepan until scalding; add sugar and salt, and stir until sugar is dissolved.

2. Whisk egg whites into yogurt; cook and stir until mixture thickens slightly and coats a spoon. Add vanilla. Chill.

3. When chilled, fold in applesauce. Whip cream until thickened and fold into mixture. Freeze for several hours or until firm.

Yield: About 8 servings.

 *FAST APPLE FAVORITE*

Apple Yogurt

1/2 cup plain yogurt
1/2 cup applesauce
1 teaspoon sugar
Nutmeg (optional)

Combine yogurt, applesauce and sugar. Sprinke with nutmeg. Good with fresh fruit, whole grain cereals or granola.

Yield: 1 cup.

Apple Fondue Fritters

1 cup pancake mix
2 tablespoons cornflake
    crumbs
1 tablespoon sugar
1/8 teaspoon curry powder
    (optional)
3/4 cup water
Vegetable oil (for frying)
4 apples, sliced
2 teaspoons cinnamon
1/2 cup sugar

1. Combine pancake mix, cornflake crumbs, 1 tablespoon sugar, and curry powder if desired. Add water and beat well until smooth. Pour batter into individual bowls and place onto the table, one for each guest.

2. Half fill a fondue pot with vegetable oil. Heat oil to 375 degrees. Place pot in the center of the table.

3. Set apple slices on the table in a plate or bowl. Mix cinnamon and sugar in a small bowl and set the bowl on the table.

4. With a fondue fork, each guest should spear an apple slice, dip it into the batter (letting excess drain into bowl), immerse the apple slice in the hot oil, and cook it for 1 to 2 minutes or until golden brown, and finally coat it with the cinnamon and sugar mixture. Repeat as desired.

Yield: 4 to 6 servings.

Note: If cornflake crumbs are not available, you can substitute finely crushed cornflakes.

Candied Apples

6 small, well-colored apples
1 cup sugar
1/2 cup water
Red food coloring (optional)

1. Remove stems from apples and insert wooden skewers in their place. (If the stems are sturdy, the apples may be candied without skewers.)

2. Cook sugar and water until brittle when tried in cold water, or until a candy thermometer registers 265 degrees. Remove from heat. Stir in a few drops of red food coloring, if desired.

3. Dip each apple into the sugar syrup, coating well. Cool on a buttered cooking sheet until coating is set.

Yield: 6 candied apples.

Adam was but human—this explains it all.
He did not want the apple for the apple's sake;
he wanted it only because it was forbidden.
Mark Twain, Pudd'nhead Wilson's Calendar

Crystallized Apple Slices

3 firm apples
1 cup sugar
1/2 cup water

1. Quarter the apples, peel, and cut each quarter into 3 slices.

2. Cook sugar and water to a syrup in small saucepan. Drop 12 apple slices into the syrup and cook slowly until transparent. Repeat until all apples are cooked.

3. Remove apple slices to wax paper and cool for 24 hours. Roll slices in sugar; repeat twice at 24-hour intervals; after the third rolling, let dry.

Yield: 36 slices.

Note: If desired, syrup may be flavored with cinnamon or mint.

Apple knockers: All persons who live west of the Hudson River and north or east of the Bronx.
Al Smith, Presidential Candidate, 1928

Old-Fashioned Apple Candy

8 large tart apples, quartered
1/2 cup water
2 cups sugar
2/3 cup red cinnamon
    candies
1 envelope unflavored
    gelatin
1/4 cup cold water
Sugar or confectioners'
    sugar

1. Cook apples, covered tightly, in 1/2 cup water until tender. Pass apples through a sieve. This should make 4 cups of applesauce.

2. Add sugar and red cinnamon candies. Simmer, uncovered, for 45 minutes.

3. Soften gelatin in 1/4 cup cold water. Add to hot mixture. Cook for 20 minutes, stirring constantly. Pour into a greased 8-inch square pan. Cool.

4. Cut into squares; dip in granulated or confectioners' sugar. Let stand for one day. Store in a cool place.

Yield: 64 pieces of candy.

Bless, oh Lord, the courage of this Prince
and prosper the works in his hands
and may his land be filled
with apples.
Ancient Saxon coronation benediction

Notes

Notes

Apple Index

A

Aeble Kage (Apple Cake), 106
All-Purpose Apple Stuffing, 65
Apple Apricot Torte, 115
Apple Baked Alaska, 145
Apple Blossom, 124
Apple Bonnie, 107
Apple Bread Pudding, 138
Apple Butter
    Vermont Apple Butter, 71
Apple Butterscotch Squares,
    128
Apple Charlotte, 137
Apple Cheese Bread, 83
Apple Cheese Cake, 108
Apple Cheese Pie, 93
Apple Cheese Tarts, 104
Apple Cheese Soufflé, 49
Apple-Cider Salad, 60
Apple Cinnamon Cheesies, 27
Apple Cobbler, 135
Apple Coffeecake, 85
Apple Cornbread, 84
Apple Crisp, 136
Apple Custard Cream Pie, 94
Apple Date Squares, 127
Apple Dipper, 17
Apple Dolmas, 46
Apple Dumplings, 125
Apple Flan, 102
Apple Fondue Fritters, 147
Apple Frozen Yogurt, 146
Apple Hermits, 129
Apple Honey-Buns, 78
Apple Indian Pudding, 141
Apple Jelly, 72
Apple and Knockwurst
    Supper, 38
Apple Kugel, 142
Apple Muffins, 89

Apple Napoleons, 118
Apple Noodle Pudding, 143
Apple Pancake, 50
Apple Pastry Logs, 119
Apple Pound Cake, 109
Apple Praline Pie, 96
Apple Raisin Braid, 77
Apple Raisin Cookies, 126
Apple and Sausage Quiche, 37
Apple Soufflé Salad, 61
Apple-Stuffed Crêpes, 132
Apple Supreme, 139
Apple Yogurt, 146
Apple-Yogurt Molded Salad,
    62
Apples on English, 47
Applesauce
    Applesauced Pork Chops,
        36
    Pam's Chocolate Birthday
        Cake, 105
    Ricotta Apple Roll-Ups,
        133
    Rosy Applesauce, 70
Applesauced Pork Chops, 36
Aunt Rashe's Streusel
    Coffeecake, 86

B

Baked Apple Coconut
    Doughnuts, 87
Baked Chicken Barbecue, 41
Baked Stuffed Acorn Squash,
    55
Banana
    Curried Apple and
        Banana Soup, 24
Barney's Hot Apple Pie, 101
Bavarian Apple Almond Torte,
    114

F

Fast Apple Favorites
  Apple Salsa Dip, 21
  Apple Yogurt, 146
  Extra-Moist Chocolate
    Cake, 112
  Stir-Fry, 47
Festive Fruit-Salad Bowl, 63
Fish
  Julia's Danish Herring, 21
Flan
  Apple Flan, 102
Fondue
  Apple Fondue Fritters, 147
Fresh Apple Mousse, 140
Fritters
  Apple Fondue Fritters, 147
Frosty Apple Salad, 64
Fruit (other than Apple)
  Apple Apricot Torte, 115
  Apple Hermits, 129
  Apple Raisin Braid, 77
  Cranberry-Glazed Cheese
    Pie, 97
  Curried Apple and
    Banana Soup, 24
  Festive Fruit-Salad Bowl,
    63
  Frosty Apple Salad, 64
  Fruit Curry Dip, 18
  Fruit Noodle Pudding, 144
  Jenny's Jellied Apple
    Salad,59
  Raisin Spice Oatmeal
    Bread,81
  Roast Lamb with Apples,
    35
  Fruit Curry Dip, 18

G

Goddess Tribute, 111
Grated Apple Meringue Pie, 98

H

Ham
  Swedish Ham Balls, 22
Hermits
  Apple Hermits, 129
Honey
  Apple Honey-Buns, 78
  Honey of an Apple Pie, 99
  Honey-Mustard Dressing,
    67
Honey of an Apple Pie, 99
Honey-Mustard Dressing, 67
Hors d'Oeuvre
  Cheese Appletizers, 20
  Julia's Danish Herring, 21
  Sausage and Apple
    Appleteasers, 19
  Swedish Ham Balls, 22
  Zesty Hors d'Oeuvre, 23

I

Indian Relish, 69

J

Jelly
  Apple Jelly, 72
Jenny's Jellied Apple Salad, 59
Jiffy Apple Stuffing, 66
Julia's Danish Herring, 21

K

Knockwurst
  Apple and Knockwurst
    Supper, 38

L

Roast Lamb with Apples, 35

M

McIntosh Country Meatloaf, 32
Meatloaf
McIntosh Country Meatloaf, 32
Mini Apple Strudels, 117
Mousse
Fresh Apple Mousse, 140
Muffins
Apple Muffins, 89
Mulled Cider, 26

N

Napoleons
Apple Napoleons, 118
New England Autumn Casserole, 56
Noodle
Apple Kugel, 142
Apple Noddle Pudding, 143
Fruit Noodle Pudding, 144

O

Old-Fashioned Apple Candy, 150
Old-Fashioned Doughnut Balls, 88

P

Pam's Chocolate Birthday Cake, 105
Pancake
Apple Pancake, 50
Pastry
Apple Flan, 102
Apple Pastry Logs, 119
Apple Napoleons, 118

Pies
Apple Cheese Pie, 93
Apple Custard Cream Pie, 94
Apple Praline Pie, 96
Barney's Hot Apple Pie, 101
Caramel Apple Pie, 95
Cranberry-Glazed Cheese Pie, 97
Grated Apple Meringue Pie, 98
Honey Apple Pie, 99
Sour Cream Apple Pie, 100
Pork
Apple and Sausage Quiche, 37
Applesauced Pork Chops, 36
Spicy Apple Ribs Country-Style, 31
Stir-Fry, 47
Puddings
Apple Bread Pudding, 138
Apple Indian Pudding, 141
Apple Kugel, 142
Apple Noodle Pudding, 143
Fruit Noodle Pudding, 144

Q

Quiche
Apple and Sausage Quiche, 37
Quick Apple Kuchen, 112
Quick Raisin Bran Bread, 82

R

Raisin
Apple Muffins, 89

Stuffing
   All-Purpose Apple
      Stuffing, 65
   Jiffy Apple Stuffing, 66
Sugar-and-Spice Pot Roast, 34
Superb Scandinavian Apple
   Soup, 25
Swedish Ham Balls, 22
Sweet Apple Bread, 79
Sweet Apple Cabbage, 57
Sweet Potato
   Sweet-Potato Scallop, 58

T

Tarts
   Apple Cheese Tarts, 104
   Apple Flan, 102
   Rickrack Apple Tart, 103
Tomato Chutney, 68
Tortes
   Apple Apricot Torte, 115
   Bavarian Apple Almond
      Torte, 114
   Goddess Tribute, 111

V

Vegetable
   Baked Stuffed Acorn
      Squash, 55
   Indian Relish, 69
   New England Autumn
      Casserole, 56
   Sweet Apple Cabbage, 57
   Sweet Potato Scallop, 58
   Tomato Chutney, 68
Vermont Apple Butter, 71
Viennese Apple Strudel, 116

Y

Yogurt
   Apple Frozen Yogurt, 146
   Apple Yogurt, 146
   Apple-Yogurt Moded
      Salad, 62

Z

Zesty Hors d'Oeuvre, 23